THE
EDUCATION
OF OUR
DESIRES

THE
EDUCATION
OF OUR
DESIRES

Marlow C. Hunter

Bridgewood Publishing
A Self-Publishing Imprint of Cedar Fort, Inc.
Springville, Utah

This is not an official publication of the Church of Jesus Christ of Latter-day Saints. The opinions and views expressed herein belong solely to the author and do not necessarily the opinions and views of the Publisher. Permission for the use of sources, graphics, and photos is also the responsibility of the author.

ISBN 13: 978-0-692-18929-0

Published by Bridgewood Publishing, a self-publishing imprint of Cedar Fort, Inc.
2373 W. 700 S. Springville, UT 84663

REL046000   RELIGION / Christianity / Church of Jesus Christ of Latter-day Saints (Mormon)
REL012070   RELIGION / Christian Life / Personal Growth
SEL032000   SELF-HELP / Spiritual

Cover design © 2018 Marlow Hunter
Edited by Catherine Christensen and Melissa Caldwell
Typeset by Sydnee Hyer

Printed in the United States of America

10 9 8 7 6 5 4 3 2 1 .

Printed on acid-free paper

CONTENTS

FOREWORD

B e ye therefore perfect."

This injunction, quoted by Matthew from the Sermon on the Mount, remains as one of the Savior's most challenging commandments uttered to his disciples. Perfection, like Godhood, seems a high, almost impossible bar to attain. Answering the question, "What did Jesus really mean here?" has haunted commentators and preachers alike for centuries. This four-word invitation has been viewed both as inspirational and intimidating. In all likelihood, no single verse in scripture has created more anxiety than this one and resulted in such widely diverse explanations. Perhaps the greatest unintended consequence of the Master's sermon is the false idea that the state of "perfection" is an event we will experience at some point in time. Yesterday I was not quite perfect—but today I finished the last requirements and now I am! And Perfection as an 'event' has a corollary: Eternal happiness is dependent on being perfect. Thus, yesterday I wasn't yet perfect or really happy. Today, I completed the last requirements and I am now perfect and happy!

Our culture has become an "events culture" because we measure our progress toward perfection by our actions/behaviors. The scriptures contain a plethora of observable benchmarks to be achieved: pay our tithes and offerings, live by the Word of Wisdom, observe the law chastity, etc. What manner of men and women we are to be is defined as being like Christ and doing what He would do. Over the years, much has been written and spoken about "perfecting" our works. We know, for instance, that certain works are absolutely mandatory, such as baptism, receiving and keeping the covenants associated with our endowments, and temple marriage. But there are many more which provide for growth and development along the covenant path; they are easily identifiable and measurable in terms of our progression toward eternal life: ministering (formerly home and visiting teaching), going to the stake welfare farm, working at the bishop's storehouse, accepting and faithfully serving in a variety of callings in the kingdom of God on the earth, to name a few. In sum, there is no shortage of guidance as to perfecting ourselves and overcoming the natural man through works.

However, from a clarifying statement in the 1836 revelation (D&C 137:9) to the Prophet Joseph in the Kirtland Temple while he was conducting certain ordinances of the endowment as far as they had been revealed at that time, we know that we will be judged by both our works and our desires. Therefore, we understand that desires have at least as much to do with our eternal destination as do works. Desires present different and perhaps more difficult challenges as we wend our way along the path toward perfection. Certainly, measuring progress is much less observable. Unlike works, which have created an "event-driven" culture, desires are far more subtle and are best associated with the notion of being "process-driven." Marking certain life events gives a sense we have arrived at a certain time and place. We have attained the moment, achievement, status, or location. From our new vantage point we can also see those who have not yet arrived. Clearly, we have experienced the event and they have not. Events are how we mark our life's progress in comparison to those around us. Paraphrasing C. S. Lewis, pride is not having so much of a thing; it is the knowing that we have more of it than someone else.

The education of our desires operates more like our natural world. We plant a seed, then nurture it, nourish it and cultivate it, until over a period of gradual change, a tree, bush or flower unfolds. Desires evolve over time, and frequently, change is often not readily observable. In addition, educating our desires is achieved through personal revelation, which is received over the course of a lifetime. Finally, comparatively little has been written or spoken about aligning our desires with those of our Heavenly Father and His Son, Jesus Christ. This book opens up the conversation about the process of educating desires by exploring the source of desires, how they can be educated, and suggesting righteous desires to be sought after, some of which we are acquainted with, but others may surface as desires we have "never supposed."

When President Joseph F. Smith suggested that our exaltation hangs on the education of our desires, I believe this is what he had in mind. Plodding through the daily muck of mortality, mercy, and kindness, at

times, may seem a foreign idea. And the journey to have our desires educated and trained and refined may seem a long journey. And yet that is
what a loving Father and Mother seek for us—a refinement of our desires,
which open the door to an eternal relationship with our Heavenly Parents,
in their presence, wanting what they want, seeking what they seek, loving
what they love. Thus, the education of our desires is of great worth to our
happiness, now and in the future. It is also worthy of our study and attention. As we do so, we come to recognize that this transforming of wants
and desires comes as a seed planted in fertile soil. They grow only as they
are nourished and nurtured (Alma 32:28). They grow because Heavenly
Father desires them to transform his children into celestial beings like
him.

As this book clearly points out, such monumental change does not
come without pain or discomfort. Our natural man and woman know
what they want. Mortality is filled with a buffet of enticements. Curbing
human appetites and passions is no small task. There is no on/off switch in
our soul that immediately turns off the cravings for things of this world.
But education, any education, is filled with lectures and homework, mid-
terms and comprehensive course finals. It comes with essay questions but
also difficult multiple choice exams where there seems to be several right
answers we must choose from. Our education will also be aided by failed
exams, lessons not learned and repeated. At those times we may be driven
to seek divine tutoring. With that additional help, we may then retake
critical tests and pass them.

The education of our desires is more than a worthy exercise—it is of
vital importance to our happiness. It is the purpose of our earthy sojourn
here. And this education has, is, and always will be provided by a loving,
merciful Teacher, bent on our success and growth.

—Kevin Hinckley

ACKNOWLEDGMENTS

This book could not have been envisioned, written, or published without the help of others.

I want to thank the wonderful people at Bridgewood Publishing for seeing something in my manuscript that prompted them to undertake this project submitted by an unknown author and for being the facilitators of helping me realize a dream. Liz Knight, Luke Selway, Emily Chambers, Catherine Christensen, Melissa Caldwell, and Sydnee Hyer have worked tirelessly and closely with me throughout the publishing process. They have done a magnificent job with the copyediting, the substantive editing, the cover design, and many other functions associated with a project of this nature that were performed behind the scenes of which I am not aware. Through all of this, they maintained a high level of professionalism in all its meanings and nuances.

Much of what is contained in this publication is a plethora of input from myriads of people that I have had the privilege and invaluable opportunity to engage in stewardship conversations as a leader and teacher in a variety of forums.

Finally, I express appreciation to my friend and colleague, Kevin Hinckley, who graciously wrote the foreword to this publication. We have shared many marvelous exchanges of ideas on multitudinous gospel and other topics for almost forty years of friendship. His encouragement and inspiration during the times of discouragement were such that this book is no longer a dream but a reality.

CHAPTER 1
Introduction

"Faith exists when absolute confidence in that which we cannot see combines with action that is in absolute conformity to the will of our Heavenly Father."

—Joseph B. Wirthlin[1]

W̲e know very little about the transition from this mortal existence to the presence of our Heavenly Parents in their royal courts on high; however, the Lord has revealed in unmistakable terms the nature of His assessment of how we will become the recipients of our eternal inheritance. We will be judged by our works and by our desires.

"For I, the Lord, will **judge** all men according to their works, **according to the desire of their hearts**." (Doctrine and Covenants 137:9)

"...For I know that he granteth unto men according to their desire..." (Alma 29:4)

"The one raised to happiness according to his desires of happiness, or good according to his desires of good..." (Alma 41:5)

"Verily, verily, I say unto you, even as you desire of me so shall it be unto you..." (Doctrine and Covenants 6:8; see also 7:8 and 11:8, 17).

"Delight thyself in the Lord; and he shall give thee the desires of thine heart" (Psalm 37:4).

Hence, fashioning our desires to "be partakers of the divine nature" (2 Peter 1:4) by realigning our wills to coincide with God's will is critical in our quest to become like Christ.

After less than twenty years of living in the promised land, Nephi found himself and his family in familiar circumstances—namely, his brothers seeking to take his (and Lehi's) life. And so, like Abraham who "saw that it was needful ... to obtain another place of residence" (Abraham 1:1), Nephi, his family, and those who desired to go with him, departed on a journey into another "wilderness." After many days of being led by the Lord, they established a new community, where they "did observe to keep the judgments, and the statutes, and the commandments of the Lord in all things, according to the law of Moses" (2 Nephi 5:10), which enabled them to live "after the manner of happiness" (2 Nephi 5:27).

We "live after the manner of happiness" when we choose to allow the Lord to educate our desires. Letting our wills be increasingly swallowed up in the will of the Father is a divine tutoring process, not an event. Lest there be trembling with the significance of process, we should remember that mortality is a continuation of our having successfully incorporating that process of exercising the "exceedingly great faith" (Alma 13:3) that was required while in our premortal home to align our desires with those of our Heavenly Father instead of Lucifer's subtle but nefarious desires. In that realm, we developed and improved upon many righteous desires, the most significant of which was the desire to become like our Heavenly Parents and our Savior, Jesus Christ, evidenced by our accepting and sustaining Heavenly Father's plan. We aligned our desires with His there and then, so we can do the same thing here and now.

Elder Neil L. Andersen taught us that "faith is not only a feeling; it is a decision."[2] Decisions are driven by and made based on the desires centered in our hearts. Mortality is the opportunity to continue to identify, select, and implement righteous desires. Ultimately, they are the only things that uniquely belong to each of us that can be placed on the altar of broken hearts and contrite spirits. We did it before; therefore, we can do it again, with the help of the Spirit. Such is the essence of worship as revealed to the Prophet Joseph: "I give unto you these sayings that you may understand and know how to worship, and know what you worship, that you may come unto the Father in my name, and in due time receive of his fulness" (Doctrine and Covenants 93:19). A prayer found in a Reform Judaism prayer book drives home this point: "The Gods we worship write their names on our faces and we will worship something. The desires which dominate our imagination and our thoughts will determine our life and character. Therefore, it behooves us to be careful what we are worshipping; for what we are worshipping, we are becoming."[3]

This book is intended to help all of us focus on those righteous desires, which will [1] result in peace of mind and soul because they will be aligned with God's desires, [2] fuel faith in Jesus Christ, and [3] cause us to live after the manner of happiness and become like our Heavenly Parents. Educating our desires is and will be a continuing challenge!

The sons of Mosiah were faced with a dilemma. They had to figure out what the Lord desired of them, especially when new desires growing in their hearts conflicted with the desire of their father, King Mosiah, who wanted them to succeed him in governing the Nephites. Following their repentance and reconversion to the gospel, Ammon, Aaron, Omner, and Himni became engaged in sincere and earnest efforts to heal the wounds they had caused to the souls of the believers in Zarahemla. While performing their restitutional labors, a new and unexpected desire was kindled in their hearts and grew from a tiny flicker to the raging flames of a burning bush. Things came to a head on the day that the four sons of Mosiah declared their intentions to undertake a mission to teach the gospel to the Lamanites in the land of Nephi. The record in the Book of Mormon describes the circumstances surrounding that announcement: "having taken leave of their father Mosiah in the first year of the judges; having refused the kingdom which their father was desirous to confer upon them" (Alma 17:6). The sons of Mosiah also faced further challenges, which could potentially undermine their desires to preach to the Lamanites, from others they knew—most likely friends and neighbors.

> Now do ye remember, my brethren, that we said unto our brethren in the land of Zarahemla, we go up to the land of Nephi, to preach to our brethren, the Lamanites, and they laughed us to scorn? For they said unto us: Do ye suppose that ye can bring the Lamanites to the knowledge of the truth? Do ye suppose that ye can convince the Lamanites of the incorrectness of the traditions of their fathers, as stiffnecked a people as they are; whose hearts delight in the shedding of blood; whose days have been spent in the grossest of iniquity; whose ways have been the ways of a transgressor from the beginning? Now, my brethren, ye remember that this was their language. (Alma 26:23–24)

Such was the difficult situation the four sons of Mosiah found themselves facing. Would they observe the fifth commandment—to honor father and mother and their noble desires—or listen to the voice of the Spirit, which had communicated a different message? Furthermore, should they succumb to the peer pressure of their "brethren" who ridiculed the foolish and absurd notion of proclaiming the gospel to such a wicked and perverse people? No doubt many of us have experienced how difficult it can be to determine what the Lord's intents are for us when we are faced with so many conflicting voices. But the sons of Mosiah had learned to distinguish the voice of the Lord, allowing them to move forward in faith to align their wills with God's.

The day after returning home from my mission, I found myself in a similar circumstance. Based on what my parents felt were righteous desires for my well-being and ultimate happiness, they shared with me their plans for my post-mission life. First, I was to return to Brigham Young University (BYU), which I had attended prior to entering the mission field, where I was to obtain a degree in secondary education. Second, I was to marry one of the daughters of their long-time best friends. Third, upon the successful completion of my studies and graduation, I was to move back to my hometown. Fourth, I was to accept a position as teacher in the public school system, which (I discovered later) had been arranged by my father based upon his friendship with the Superintendent of Schools.

Needless to say, I was in "no man's land." What was I supposed to do? Were my parents' desires in alignment with Heavenly Father's desires for me? What would be the consequences, both for me and for my parents, of not doing what they desired? Over the course of time during which I was completing my college degree, it became clear as to what God wanted me to do. Of the four courses of actions outlined by my parents, I only followed the first one. I completed my education at BYU (but did not earn a degree in secondary education). However, I did not marry the daughter of their close friends. I did not move back to my hometown, and I did not become a teacher in the public education system.

"Rejecting" three of the four desires my parents outlined that day was tough. Just like King Mosiah, my father and mother were faithful Latter-day Saints who had served the Lord in many capacities. I am sure that it was painful for them to accept that I decided to go in a different direction. The desires of Heavenly Father were tailored to groom me to become a servant that He needed in another part of His vineyard. It took many years, during which my parents continued to try and persuade me to move back to my hometown, abandon my chosen profession, and take a job in the public education system, before they eventually acknowledged that my desires, priorities, choices, and decisions turned out to be the best for my life. The spectrum of our desires runs the gamut. For instance, many of us desire our lives to turn out a certain way and are disappointed when they don't. Consider the closing scene of a television drama, which occurs in a cemetery where confusion and purposelessness is poignantly lamented by one of the characters:

> Are all men's lives broken and tumultuous, agonized and unromantic, punctuated by screams and shedding of tears, agonies, and death? Who knows? ... I don't know.... WHY CAN'T PEOPLE HAVE WHAT THEY WANT? The things were all there to content everybody, yet everybody got the wrong thing.[4]

On the other hand, some who do get what they want in life discover that their desires have been hollow, lacking in substance and meaning. They further come to realize that the ladder of success they are climbing is leaning on the wrong wall. Consider the haunting explanation of Jacob, brother of Nephi:

> The Jews... sought for things that they could not understand. ... God hath taken away his plainness from them, and delivered unto them many things which they cannot understand, because they desired it. And *because they desired it*, God hath done it..." (Jacob 4:14, emphasis added)

In sum, many of us desire our lives to turn out a certain way, and they don't. Sadly, they come to realize that when their desires are seen as they truly are (Doctrine and Covenants 93:24), they are not what they really wanted. Is it possible that we don't really know for certain what it is we should want or desire? It is a circumstance equivalent to Paul's counsel to the Romans about prayer; "for we know not what we should pray for as we ought" (Romans 8:26). Thus, it behooves each of us to find out what our desires should be, and then be willing to jettison those desires that are not in harmony with Heavenly Father's plan. While it is true that God "granteth unto men [and women] according to their desire" (Alma 29:4), we also need to learn to pray for "the things we ought," and submit to God's curriculum of educating our desires so that they will align with

His desires. Our objective should be to arrive at the point of being able to say, "All I want is what You (Heavenly Father) want."

One purpose of this book is to help readers come to understand that Heavenly Father's desires trump all others. During mortality, there is a divinely designed tutorial process to educate our desires so that, at the completion of our mortal probation, we will have incorporated righteous desires into the fabric of our souls, and inherit the ultimate happiness prepared for us. Most, if not all of us, ponder at various stages of our lives, and wonder why things have not turned out the way we expected or planned. This book defines the process of having our desires educated by examining real-life examples of making choices. It also illustrates a number of righteous desires that can serve as stimuli for us to ponder as we identify, select, and act on in our lives. The reader will discover ideas that will help us to "be about [our] Father's business" (Luke 2:49). The greater our desires, the greater will be our motivation; and the greater the motivation, the greater the achievement.

Elder Neal A. Maxwell's book *That Ye May Believe*[5] is a collection of letters sent to his twenty (at the time) grandchildren discussing pertinent gospel topics that he believed would help each one individually. The letter written to his grandson Jacob particularly caught my attention. It was titled "Educating our Desires." (The entire text of the letter can be found in Chapter 3.) Its message was powerful, particularly the opening line, which quoted President Joseph F. Smith: "You and I must take great care concerning the education of our desires." Without question, this prophetic statement emphasizes the importance of desires and that they need to be educated. This leaves us with the issue of how to accomplish that. In our church lives, we frequently define and measure our gospel progress in terms of "events-oriented" activities (e.g., baptism and confirmation, priesthood ordinations, going on missions, being married in the temple). These are all appropriate and good. But as has been mentioned above and will be discussed at length below, our eternal destiny is also a function of our desires, the education of which is "process-oriented."

Paul taught the Corinthians a new paradigm, namely that although parts of the body come in two varieties—comely and uncomely—they are to be accorded different levels of honor. We recall that the Greeks were body-worshippers.

> Nay, much more those members of the body, which seem to be more feeble are necessary: And those members of the body, which we think

to be less honorable, upon these we bestow more abundant honour; and our *uncomely parts have more abundant comeliness.* For our comely parts have no need [of honor]; but God hath tempered the body together, having given *more abundant honour to that part which lacked.* (1 Corinthians 12:22–24, emphasis added)

Paul's analogy of the significance of body parts can be applied to the process of educating our desires. Clearly, certain desires tend to grab the headlines and bright neon lights, but we should bestow honor and devote efforts to develop a plethora of less comely desires. What are some of the uncomely desires that are also righteous which should receive more attention? What about unrighteous desires? What are the sources of our desires, both righteous and unrighteous? How does the Lord educate our desires? What is the "educational" objective of educating our desires?

What follows is my humble effort to share my thoughts and understandings relative to educating our desires in the hopes that those who read this book will come away with a different paradigm of understanding, not only our glamorous desires, but also, more important, we will find additional motivation to gather and nurture uncomely but godly and powerful desires that are not advertised with fireworks and glitz. Rather, such desires are heard and felt through the power and promptings of the Holy Ghost. My desire for you, the reader, is that what is contained herein will inspire you to identify, assess, and educate your desires. So much has been spoken and written about our works and their impact on Judgment Day, that it seems appropriate to have a discussion about the role of our desires. After all, in the grand scheme of Father's plan, they really do matter and should be educated in the manner prescribed by the Lord as our tutor and given more abundant honor. To manifest our heart's desires, we must be willing to be and do what our Heavenly Father desires. And we must learn to trust God with the timing of the desires of our hearts. Paraphrasing President George Albert Smith, "it is our duty, first of all, to learn what the Lord wants" (aka His desires).[6] We cannot possibly align our desires with His, unless we find out what the Lord's desires are for each of us.

Notes

1. Joseph B. Wirthlin, "Shall He Find Faith on the Earth?" *Ensign,* Nov. 2002.

2. Neil L. Andersen, "It's True, Isn't It? Then What Else Matters?" *Ensign*, May 2007.
3. Avodat Halev, *Worship of the Heart*, Issac M. Wise Temple, K. K. B'Nai Yeshurun, Cincinnati, Ohio, 2008, p. 80.
4. "The Good Soldier," a television dramatization of the novel by Ford Madox Ford, Project Gutenberg EBook, January 26, 2013)
5. Neil A. Maxwell, *That Ye May Believe* (Salt Lake City, Bookcraft, Inc. 1992).
6. George Albert Smith, *Conference Report*, April 1942, 14.

CHAPTER 2
The Tutorial Curriculum

"You and I must take great care concerning the education of our desires."

—Joseph F. Smith[1]

Statesman turned prophet, Alma the Elder, sheds a ray of eternal light on God's ways and thoughts when he poured out his soul concerning his wants and desires to be of service to his Lamanite brethren and sisters: "For I know that he [God] granteth unto men according to their *desire*, whether it be unto death or unto life; yea, I know that he allotteth unto men, yea, decreeth unto them decrees which are unalterable, according to their *wills*, whether they be unto salvation or unto destruction" (Alma 29:4; emphasis added). On another occasion, this same Alma counseled his son Corianton concerning the impact our desires have on restoration and judgment.

> And it is requisite with the justice of God that men should be judged according to their works; and if their works were good in this life, and *the desires of their hearts were good*, that they should also, at the last day, be restored unto that which is good. And if their works are evil they shall be restored unto them for evil. Therefore all things shall be restored in their proper order....the one raised to happiness *according to his desires of happiness, or good according to his desires of good*; and the other to evil according to his desires of evil (Alma 41:3–5; emphasis added)

Alma teaches us and his son that our eternal destiny depends not only on our doing good works ("events"), but also educating (meaning

9

to discover what God's desires are) our desires, especially those related to happiness and goodness. Being restored, as Alma taught Corianton, means that we will become unfallen, completed, and finished (i.e. perfect) not only because we have done the "works of Abraham" (Doctrine and Covenants 132:32) but also because our desires will perfectly align with the cosmic desires of our Father in Heaven.

Early on in the Restoration, the Prophet Joseph was instructed in a revelation given in the Kirtland Temple on January 21, 1836, "For I, the Lord, will judge men according their works, *according to desire of their hearts*" (Doctrine and Covenants 137:9; emphasis added). Unmistakably, our desires carry tremendous significance in the eternal scheme of things. In an address to students at the University of Utah Institute of Religion, Elder Neal A. Maxwell,[2] reinforces how important our desires are.

> Our desires stir us deeply… desires are a profound part of our personality. They lie at the very root of our being… our deeds and our actions become an extension of those desires… We become the composite of our desires. The continuing education of our desires and the alignment of those desires with the desires of our Father in Heaven become the great challenges of education for us.

Then Elder Maxwell uttered this prophetic and sobering warning:

> Unless we align our desires with those of the Lord, we will have neither happiness here nor everlasting joy in the world to come. If we, like Abraham of old, desire even greater happiness, then we too must also be desirous of being further instructed in the ways of the Lord and in the grammar of the gospel. If we have the desire to be instructed, then we will have the patience to outlast life's seemingly imponderables and seeming contradictions.

Finally, Elder Maxwell added apostolic perspective:

> In perhaps the most significant dimension of desire, we must be willing to submit to our Father in Heaven even in those moments when He desires us to be righteously independent in making some of life's most difficult decisions, in order that we will develop our capacity to act for ourselves under the influence of His spirit and to be His friend in all circumstances… President Brigham Young said that "you and I must learn to be righteous in the dark"…and that requires us to desire to be tutored by circumstances that cause wrenching of the soul.

Given the monumental role played by our desires, it is no wonder that President Joseph F. Smith declared, "You and I must take great care concerning the education of our desires."[3] So where do our desires originate? Where do they reside? How do we identify, pursue, cultivate, and ultimately implement righteous desires? How do we recognize, repent of, and rid our souls of having unrighteous desires? Is there a hierarchy of righteous desires, just as there is "glory of the sun, moon and stars?" Are there priorities that should be assigned to the education of our desires? Are there times and places for certain desires to come to fruition? How do we help children learn about desires? How do we communicate the importance of desires to teenagers?

As with all gospel principles that impact salvation and exaltation, the Lord has revealed principles and practices to help us while in our mortal probation as we learn of his ways and thoughts which are not our ways and thoughts (see Isaiah 55:8–9). I cite two examples of the role of desires as recorded in scriptural records. First, Abraham desired changes in his life that would result in obtaining greater knowledge, greater righteousness, and greater happiness. "And, finding that there was greater happiness in peace and rest for me, I sought the blessings of the fathers... having been myself a follower of righteousness, *desiring* also to be one who possessed great knowledge, and to be a greater follower of righteousness, and to possess greater knowledge,... and desiring to receive instructions" (Abraham 1:2, emphasis added). Note Abraham's humility to not only recognize but also to acknowledge that achieving his desires would of necessity involve an ongoing instructional process, not just a singular event. Teaching moments would certainly be a reality—sacrificing Isaac comes to mind. But learning God's ways involves more than the experiments in our earthly laboratory.

Second, Nephi was impressed by knowledge that was revealed to Lehi about things that matter. Nephi desired to know more about the Lord's great plan of salvation. "For it came to pass after I had *desired* to know the things that my Father had seen, and believing that the Lord was able to make them known unto me, as I sat pondering in mine heart" (1 Nephi 11:1, emphasis added).

Nephi had learned that pondering (a process that occurs over the course of time, not a moment-in-time event) contributed to the rise and development of the desire to know the things that Lehi had seen. I am sure that Nephi's vision did not come the day after his father's vision.

Desires, Priorities, Choices, and Decisions

Our deepest desires give rise to priorities, which then define a group of options and choices from which we make decisions. Such decisions ultimately control the consequences that will be felt, both in this life and in the life to come. If our decisions align with God's will, we will exhibit godlike behaviors with all the attendant blessings and joys. On the other hand, if our decisions do not align with God's will, our behavior will be contrary to the plan of happiness. We will come to realize one day that our desires are truly our own and cannot be implanted from outside by anybody—even God—without violating the priceless God-given gift of individual moral agency. We are free to choose good or evil thus reflecting the desires spoken of by Alma. It would appear that, based on what the Lord taught Alma, "even if [we] can no more than desire to believe" (Alma 37:27), we initiate and develop desires. Desires are not something that can be developed within us against our will. Elder Maxwell postulates a working definition of desire:

> Desires characterize our very inmost feelings as representing the distillation of our strongest motivations and as that which truly calls the cadence for our thoughts, and our deeds... indeed, our desires clearly control the tilt of our souls.[4]

He then provides a rationale as to why we "must to take great care concerning the education of our desires":

- Our deepest desires control our choices; our choices then govern the consequences that will surely follow, both in this life and in the life to come.

- Desires are a profound part of our personality. They lie at the very root of our being. Therefore, our deeds and actions become the composite and extension of our desires.

- The continuing education of our desires and the alignment of those desires with the desires of our Heavenly Father becomes the great challenge of our mortal curriculum. We must first determine God's desires for us (particularly through personal prayer, scripture study, and attending the temple regularly) and then willingly participate in the lifelong learning process to align our desires with His. It can never be the other way around. There is no pain-free way for the natural man to be realigned with God; and that is one important reason why we must deeply desire to be like Him.

- If we, like Abraham of old, desire even greater happiness, then we too must be desirous of being instructed in the ways of the Lord. We must seek to comprehend not only the structure of the plan of salvation but also its substance, including the schooling that must come to each of us concerning the wintry doctrines of the gospel, such as those concerning the role of adversity and affliction.

- When we have a genuine desire for God to instruct and tutor us, as He has with so many of His children, then either the onrushing and sometimes crushing events of life or its deceptive ordinariness or perhaps in our myopic view, unfairness, will be seen realistically and developmentally.

- We should desire to develop the kind of trust and sophistication that will enable us to not mistake imperfections in each other or in the institution of the Church as being imperfections in God or in His plan.

- Thus, if people desire, really desire to believe in the Lord, to give up their seats in the synagogue if necessary, they will desire to behave in the manner which replaces the natural man with the "man of Christ." We ought not to be so surprised that once a person's false theology comes tumbling down, so does their "enemy to God" behavior. One of the characteristics about the "strait and narrow" path is that there are no corners to be cut when it comes to educating our desires.

- Constantly, all around us there are people settling for less than they are, for less than they have the possibility to become. I believe that so much of that stems from an intrinsic failure to properly educate our desires and live below our privileges.[5]

Our desires also control the degree of divine disclosure that will be given us in the Lord's time.

Yea, after having been favored above every other nation, kindred, tongue, or people; *after having all things made known unto them according to their desires*, and their faith, and prayers, of that which has been, and which is, and which is to come. (Alma 9:20, emphasis added)

An All-Inclusive "Desires" Checklist Does Not Exist

In the spirit of the words of one of our latter-day hymns, it is my desire to share with you those feelings that are in my heart that will "forge our souls in living fire, shape them to Thy great desire."[6] No doubt some well-intentioned readers will want to make a list of the desires enumerated herein and convert them into an "appendix" to be attached to that widely-prevalent "things-I-gotta-do-before-I-die" checklist stored on electronic devices for quick and easy reference, detailing all the "events" that must be completed in order to be admitted as a permanent resident of the celestial kingdom.

I am reminded of an account shared by Robert L. Millet, Emeritus Professor of Religion at Brigham Young University, who, when serving as a bishop, told of a couple who had arranged for an interview with him. The husband, in a well-rehearsed manner, reviewed all of his church-related accomplishments, which he had obviously memorized by heart from having regularly "checked" his progress by ticking off the standard LDS "life events" that constituted (for him) milestones along the straight and narrow path to the gates of the celestial kingdom. Included in is this recitation were baptism at eight years old, being ordained to the Aaronic Priesthood at twelve, and progressing every two years from deacon, to teacher, to priest; then came the call to serve a full-time mission with the accompanying ordination as an elder in the Melchizedek Priesthood; temple marriage to his sweetheart; and, finally, the arrival of children who were being raised in the patterns of the checklist, with every effort being made to ensure that they would follow the same path as their father. Not to be outdone, the wife proudly recounted her baptism, her progress awards through the Young Women's program, service as a full-time missionary, and so on. Taking a breath, they lamented by chorusing together, "We've completed all the items on the checklist. Now what?"[7]

Sadly, measuring ourselves as upstanding members of The Church of Jesus Christ of Latter-day Saints has somehow become equated with completing a series of events rather than recognizing that becoming Christ-like celestial beings requires an on-going educational process to fashion our desires to become what God desires, which in turn, leads to worthy works. This good brother and sister missed the whole purpose of preparing for and performing gospel's events. There are innumerable righteous desires, some of which are discussed herein. But I plead with readers to not transcribe the desires mentioned herein to "a new, inspired version of a gospel checklist" maintained on a social media device. The intent of this writing is to provide encouragement, insight, and greater comprehension of the process of identifying, developing, and nurturing righteous desires in to worthy actions that ultimately result in godlike behavior, with the final outcome being that we have become like Him. Further, the reader should come to recognize that the education of our desires does not end when we leave this frail existence. Upon passing through death's door, new vistas of understanding will expand our myopic view, illuminating an unseen portion of the spectrum of God's desires that we previously didn't (and couldn't) begin to contemplate.

Aligning our desires with those magnificent, multi-dimensional, and multi-faceted and holy objectives is a continuing element of our eternal progression. I plead with you that you will not become discouraged or depressed or have feelings of "having missed out"—a tragedy and certainly unintended consequence of our social media world. Do not say to yourself, "Why didn't I think of that" or "There are so many desires that I have not recognized" or "I am in third grade and so many others are in twelfth grade of the curriculum." My objective is to provide stimuli that enable you to determine what righteous desires for you are in line with His will. We should earnestly seek the inspiration of the Holy Ghost as we identify and pursue righteous desires. Much like Moses, who upon seeing the vision of all of God's creations uttered the truly humble words, "which thing I never had supposed" (Moses 1:10), desires will arise that we may never have supposed.

What I Desire for You

Through His Spirit, the Lord will educate us to find and magnify righteous desires, while purging and discarding unrighteous desires. Such efforts may require a paradigm shift in attitudes and behavior. Recall the children of Israel on the shores of the Red Sea. As they could see and no doubt hear the chariots of Pharaoh barreling toward them with certain destruction seemingly only moments away, the tribal leaders shook in fear and suggested to Moses that the camp should turn to the left or to the right, even though they had no idea what lay ahead if they went in either of those directions. Moreover, others voiced suggestions that had already sorrowed Moses's ears—"Let's go back that we may serve the Egyptians, 'for it had been better for us to serve the Egyptians, than we should die in the wilderness'" (Exodus 14:12). No one had considered walking into the sea.

Sadly, we approach many of our decisions in that manner. We study out only those items on our list of options (this is known as "paralysis by analysis"), never seeking to determine through prayer and personal revelation if the Lord has other options for us to consider. My sincere desire is that you will let the Spirit reveal to you desires that may not have been on your list of possibilities and perhaps restore several you may have crossed off believing that they could never come to pass, or some that could be expanded and added upon.

Educating Our Desires Is a Process

Once we receive divine understanding about our desires that need to be aligned with God's, it does not mean that the pathway is smooth; rather, it is filled with rocks and holes, twists and turns, sloping inclines and declines that require us to navigate with our celestial map. Unlike the time-specific gospel events in our lives, educating our desires is a restorative process, not an event. Such refining will not be totally and successfully completed in mortality. Desires are slippery "critters" influenced by our environment, culture, family, friends, and a multitude of other stimuli surrounding us in our fallen state. Sorting through, identifying, and refining our righteous desires can be a daunting task. This vital process takes time. We must be patient and willing to sacrifice, walk without a full understanding, and trust that God will reward our efforts. President Brigham Young understood the challenges faced in connection with educating righteous desires and jettisoning unrighteous desires:

> After all that has been said and done, after He has led His people for so long, do you not perceive that there is a lack of confidence in our God? Can you perceive it in yourselves? You may ask, "Brother Brigham, do you perceive it in yourself?" I do. I can see that I lack confidence, to some extent, in Him whom I trust. WHY? Because I have not the power, in consequence of that which the Fall has brought upon me...Something rises up within me, at times, that...*draws a dividing line between my interest (desires) and the interest (desires) of my Father in Heaven*; something that makes my interest and the interest of my Father in Heaven not precisely one... We should feel and understand, as far as possible, as far as fallen nature will let us, as far as we can get faith and knowledge to understand ourselves, *that the interest of that God whom we serve is our interest, and that we have no other, neither in time nor in eternity.*[8]

Eradicating the dividing line between our interests and our Heavenly Father's interest has been, is, and will continue to be a sublime and tender mercy of our Father teaching us His thoughts and His ways. No one ever said that the forging and transforming of our desires to align with God's would be easy; only that it would be worth it.

A Watchword about Unrighteous and Unproductive Desires

It almost goes without saying that there are probably as many unrighteous desires as there are righteous desires. Knowing the truth of "things as they really are" [Jacob 4:13] forewarns us about the dangers when dealing with desires. The saga of Lehi's family being asked to leave Jerusalem, which for them was the home base of the kingdom of God, is a primer on how the Lord fashions our desires to align with His. Slightly more than 10 percent of the total pages in the Book of Mormon illustrate principles of educating desires as the Lord leads a family from the Holy City (a symbol for pre-earth life) through a wilderness experience (a symbol for earth life), to a promised land (a symbol for the celestial kingdom).

For example, when commanded to build a ship, Nephi's response could have been "Yes, we will leave this land Bountiful which thou hath prepared that we might not perish (1 Nephi 17:5), just provide us with the ship like you gave us the Liahona." Or alternatively, "I will go and build the ship which thou commanded me to construct (even though I have never done anything like this before), just provide me with the tools that I will need." Elder L. Tom Perry wisely counseled us,

> I have sometimes wondered what would have happened if Nephi had asked the Lord for tools [or a completed ship] instead of a place to find the ore to make the tools. I doubt that the Lord would have honored Nephi's request [desire].[9]

We sometimes approach educating our desires in a similar fashion. We sometimes think that we have identified the proper curriculum and learning techniques that will instruct our desires to achieve optimal results. But as is often the case, our ways are not God's ways. His ways are higher than our ways (see Isaiah 55:8–9). Optimal outcomes are achieved when we follow His customized and inspired construction blueprints.

Another desire-alignment moment occurred for Lehi and his family after they had complied with the commandment to build the ship. They wanted to take certain goods and supplies with them. But the Lord had a different plan.

And it came to pass that the voice of the Lord came unto my Father that we should arise and go down into the ship...and on the morrow *after we had prepared all things...and provisions according to that which the Lord had commanded us,* we did go down into the ship... (1 Nephi 18:5–6, emphasis added).

The implications from these verses are that the Lord had identified those things that were to be loaded onto the ship; and that there were certain things which the family may have desired to take with them but which were not on "His list" and were not to be taken with them.

President Heber J. Grant wrote: "The education of our desires is one of far-reaching importance to our happiness in life...God's ways of educating our desires are, of course, always the most perfect..."[10] This principle was ratified in my life on the occasion of participating in a disciplinary council for a Melchizedek Priesthood holder who had been endowed and married in the temple. He was called before the council for having engaged in a series of serious acts unbecoming a priesthood bearer. As he recounted his activities to the members of the stake presidency and high council, it became apparent that he desired to be excommunicated so that he could continue in this inappropriate behavior. He wanted to be free from the accountability that accompanies the covenants which he had made. After a period of deliberation, the stake president announced that this brother was to be dis-fellowshipped—a decision that was ratified by unanimous vote of the members of the council.

When this good brother was called back into the room and told of the decision, he was stunned, in a state of shock. He looked like the football coach who had just been doused with the ice-water bucket. The stake president outlined a number of conditions associated with being in the dis-fellowshipped status. He would continue to be a member of the Church and therefore under the obligations of his baptismal and other covenants. He was to adhere to the oath and covenant associated with his ordination to the office of elder in the Melchizedek Priesthood and was to conduct himself accordingly. He was to rededicate himself to abiding by the covenants make in the temple—both the endowment and the celestial marriage sealing.

My understanding of the love the Lord has for each of His children was deepened as I witnessed this brother contemplating this unexpected outcome. Truly, the Lord was not punishing, even though his transgressions were many and serious. He was extending His arms of love, inviting this brother to re-embrace the gospel's truths and patterns of behavior. Typical of most dis-fellowshipment outcomes, the time period was for a year, during which he was to meet regularly with his bishop and the stake president. I don't know if this decision had the desired effect on the brother and his conduct, because I moved from the stake before a year had passed. However, I am absolutely certain that God's way of educating the desires of this brother was perfect.

The question for each of us is not just will we attend class sessions, but will we do the homework? Will we put in the time and effort in the lab with specific projects? Paul gives us wise counsel to shape our attitude and determination to be persistent "doing the will of God from the heart" (Ephesians 6:6). The Lord's tutoring methods are inconvenient, often arriving at unexpected times; they present difficulties which initially seem insurmountable; and they typically require a demolition of our current framework of desires, which were built with our myopic perspectives, and a construction of a new desires, which like Nephi's ship was built not "after the manner of men" (1 Nephi 18:2).

Notes

1. Joseph F. Smith, *Gospel Doctrine* (Salt Lake City: Deseret Book, 1939), 197.

2. Neal A Maxwell, "The Education of Our Desires," University of Utah Institute of Religion Devotional, 5 January 1983; transcribed by Daniel R. Mower.

3. Joseph F. Smith, *Gospel Doctrine*, Salt Lake City: Deseret Book, 1966, 297.

4. Neal A Maxwell "The Education of Our Desires" University of Utah Institute of Religion Devotional, 5 January 1983; transcribed by Daniel R. Mower.

5. Ibid.

6. "God of Power, God of Right," *Hymns*, No. 20.

7. Personal notes from Education Week.

8. Deseret News, September 10, 1859, 212; emphasis added.

9. L. Tom Perry, "Becoming Self Reliant," *Ensign*, Nov. 1991, 64.

10. Heber J. Grant, *Juvenile Instructor*, July 1, 1903, 400; emphasis added.

CHAPTER 3
Educating Our Desires: A Primer

Such education can lead to sanctification until "holy desires produce corresponding outward works."

—Brigham Young[1]

To begin our discussion of the process of how the Lord will educate our desires, let me share the letter written by Elder Maxwell to his grandson:

Dear Jacob,

How, you inquire, can we better "educate our desires" as President Joseph F. Smith urged? Doing this is a tall order. So much could be said about it. However, since this is being written aloft in an airplane, and on a short flight, a few comments must suffice for now. One little-used way of more honestly testing the correctness of our desires is to place those desires more honestly and specifically before God in reverent, personal prayer. Why so? Because if we are too embarrassed to petition Him concerning our desires, this will quickly confirm their incorrectness! Desires not worthy of asking Him for in help in achieving them are unworthy of us as well. Obviously, such desires should not be further nurtured in our hearts and our minds.

Alas, some of us nurse certain desires secretly which would involve breaking God's commandments to some degree. Hence, instead we pray to God over our "safe" agendum, rather than asking Him for help in dismissing our dangerous (unrighteous) desires. Since He knows of those errant, secret desires anyway, we ought to ask for His help in dismissing them. Basically; however, we can educate our desires only as we learn more about what God's desires for us are. Since He is perfect in knowledge and love, we can trust Him to desire what is best for us—now and forever. This is part of coming to have the "mind of Christ," which facilitates our developing His desires within in us. (See I Corinthians 2:16)[2]

Prayer seems to be the catalyst that causes various tutorial ingredients to combine producing the optimal education of our desires. However, I hasten to add that receiving the answers being sought is not about saying the right words; rather, it entails developing the right heart. Prayer is the conduit for necessary and vital personal revelation that is essential not only to our survival, as President Nelson has emphasized on multiple occasions, but also to the salvational progress along the covenant path. His Imperial Majesty Emperor Haile Salassie I set forth our objective when offering petitions to heaven—"Man desires many things, but it is the individual's duty and responsibility to desire the proper things."

After reading this letter, I was reminded of an incident from the Old Testament involving Hannah and her desire to have a son. To be able to bear children was a frequent and sincere request made to the Lord, not in vain repetition, but at appropriate times by more than one daughter of God. Hannah's faith-filled requests were eventually answered with the arrival of Samuel. However, the message for us is not just that Hannah entered into a sacred covenant arising from her desires to have a child, but rather it is that her longed-for desire was in accordance with God's desire for her. The record indicates that Eli, the officiating priest, was sitting in the temple and saw Hannah. Based on his observations of her actions, he concluded she was drunk and rebuked her. In almost an unheard of response (Jewish women never addressed the Levite priests or temple workers), Hannah gathered the fortitude to reply with courage and conviction and explained that she had been pouring out her soul to the Lord to remove her barrenness (see 1 Samuel 1:13–16).

What gave Hannah strength to speak up as she did? I believe it is likely that Hannah had already prayed and received confirmation from God that her "plan" to give her son to God (should she be blessed to conceive and deliver a son) was a proper desire and totally in accordance with God's interest (desire). Thus her righteous desire filled her with the strength to testify to Eli, who was so moved by her sincere commitment that he said, "Go in peace; and the God of Israel grant thee thy petition that thou has asked of him" (1 Samuel 1:17).

Hannah had prayed to know the Lord's will before she had prayed about her own desires, so she already knew that her desire to have a son and dedicate him to the Lord's service was righteous. The relevant message for us is that before we pray for a certain desired blessing, we may want to find out if what we want is what God wants. Most of us who listen for and seek to live by the Spirit are fairly confident that we know what we want. But are the things that we want what God wants? Making assumptions can be hazardous to our well-being. It could also be a huge waste of our time, energies, and talents.

Educating our desires always involves prayer to determine if our desires align with God's. "Prayer is the act by which the will of the Father and the will of the child are brought into correspondence with each other. The object of prayer is not to change the will of God, but to secure for ourselves and for others blessings that God is already willing to grant but that are made conditional on our asking for them."[3] I recall one of my learning moments while serving as a young bishop. My business partner expected me to work some evenings and some Saturdays (especially during income tax filing season—professionally I am a CPA) in order to not work on Sundays given my many responsibilities associated with the Sabbath day. Late one such Saturday evening, I was at my office working when I received a phone call from a very concerned brother who lived in a distant city requesting that I go to the hospital located a few blocks from my office and give his ninety-year-old father-in-law (whom I will call Brother Ferguson) a priesthood blessing to be healed. Looking at my watch, I noted it was nearly 10:00 p.m. In spite of the lateness of the hour, I agreed to go. I then called my high priest group leader who fortuitously was a physician with rights at this particular small, private hospital. He said he would meet me there and arrange for clearance to go into ICU, since I was not a family member.

As I drove to the hospital, I reviewed in my mind the procedure associated with sealing an administration of consecrated oil for healing of those in special need. I remember thinking of some appropriate words to say that, in essence, would be asking the Lord to bless this faithful brother (whom I had known for a long time) to be restored to health with the able assistance of those in the medical professional who were treating him. I parked my car and went in to find the ICU and the high priest group leader. I did not mention that my desires were to pronounce a blessing of healing. Brother Ferguson had a large family, being the patriarch over many sons, daughters, grandchildren, and great-grandchildren. How could I not bless him with anything short of a recovery so as to remain in mortality with his loved ones?

The anointing having been performed in accordance with Church procedures by the high priest group leader, I then laid my hands on Brother Ferguson's head to seal the anointing and to pronounce a blessing. The instant I did so, a voice distinctly whispered to me, "Do not say or imply in any way that Brother Ferguson will be healed!" The inspiration was clear and emphatic! My desire to pronounce a blessing for a complete recovery was *not* in line with God's desires. Brother Ferguson was being called home. I learned the next morning that he had slipped quietly into the spirit world around 3:00 a.m. I learned a great lesson that, as a bishop, I needed to be sure my desires were His desires. I also learned that promptings should be acted on without thought or worry about the consequences. For a few moments, I must confess, I considered what certain family members who were not active in the Church might say when the blessing they desired and thought that as the Lord's spokesperson I would pronounce did not come to fruition.

Like Hannah, our first prayer should be to determine if our desires are righteous and in His interest, *before* we ask for the specific, desired blessing. All too often, we ask Heavenly Father to grant us certain blessings, but it never crosses our minds to find out first if that blessing we believe (or assume) to be a righteous desire is actually in harmony with God's desires. It could turn out not to be the case or not to be at the right time.

Given the significance of educating our desires, how does this process occur? May I offer several suggestions? First, the Holy Ghost, who has many vital roles in the great plan of happiness, is most likely the best starting point. Elder Orson Pratt of the Twelve wrote the following about one of those roles:

> Baptism of fire and the Holy Ghost cleanses more thoroughly, by renewing the inner man, and by purifying the affections, desires, and thoughts which have long been habituated in the impure ways of sin. Without the power of the Holy Ghost, a person...would have but very little power to change...and to walk in the newness of life... Hence, it

is infinitely important that the affections and DESIRES should be, in a measure, changed and renewed, so as to cause him to hate that which he before loved, and to love that which he before hated; thus to renew the mind of man is the work of the Holy Ghost.[4]

The Holy Ghost is the vehicle by which the atoning power of Jesus Christ is made efficacious in our lives on a daily basis as we operate under the influence of our heart's desires. What better educator of our desires could there be than the Comforter Jesus promised to send: "But the Comforter, which is the Holy Ghost, whom the Father will send in my name, he shall teach you all things" (John 14:26). Each of us should have the desire to be schooled by the Holy Ghost. However, in order for that to happen, we must first reject the notion described by Freidrich Nietzsche: "People don't want to hear the truth because they do not want their illusions destroyed." If our desire is not to accept the truths taught by the Holy Ghost, then none will be forthcoming. It's like what a wonderful friend who is also a motivational speaker regularly proclaims, "You gotta wanna!" We must put first things first and begin the education of our desires at the center of our hearts, which is where desires reside. The words of Brigham Young bring great comfort and assurance:

> If we are enjoying the Gift of the Holy Ghost in our lives—that is, if we have what Paul called "the earnest promise of the Spirit" or the "earnest of our inheritance" (2 Corinthians 1:22, 5:5, Ephesians 1:14)—then we have God's sweet certification that we are on "saving ground," that we are living in what might be called a saved condition, and that if our lives were to be interrupted by death, we would enjoy an entrance into paradise and eventually into the highest heaven.[5]

What is the objective of educating our desires? Put succinctly, to become "unfallen." The gospel is not just series of "to do's" on some mythical eternal checklist. Elder David A. Bednar reminds us, "Simply performing and dutifully checking off all the things on our lengthy gospel 'to do' list does not necessarily enable us to receive His image on our countenance or bring about the mighty change of heart [described in Alma 5:14]."[6] The gospel is not a prescription that will prevent us from doing bad things. We are to do the "works of Abraham" (John 8:39); but doing those works must result in grace, obtained freely from the Savior, changing us so that we become like our Father in Heaven, particularly changing us so that our desires become aligned with His desires.

Desire to Retain Our Inheritance

During the course of my professional career as a CPA, I learned a true but tragic economic principle. There is a rule of thumb among CPAs who work with estate and inheritance situations with which I initially disagreed. However, as time went by and I gained experience, I came to accept it as being an accurate maxim. In most situations, inheritances are gone within eighteen months of being received as a bequest (gift) from someone's will. No, there is not a "rainy day" savings account; no, there are not funded 529 plans to help pay for the continuing escalation of the cost for a college education of either children or grandchildren. The inheritance has been spent, reminiscent of the prodigal son who "took his journey into a far country, and there wasted his substance [inheritance] with riotous living" (Luke 15:13).

On a positive note, there are many circumstances where inheritances were wisely used to pay-off seemingly insurmountable mountains of debt such as credit cards, student loans, car loans, and so on. However, whether put to good use or spent frivolously, in most cases, funds received from someone's estate are gone in eighteen months. Let me now make gospel application.

It is vital to remember that similar to our mortal world, an inheritance is a specific bequest put in a will in writing from someone else. We do not *earn* an inheritance. It comes as a *gift*, as taught in what is just a partial listing of scriptural teachings—

"He that putteth his trust in me...shall inherit my holy mountain" (Isaiah 57:13)

"Knowing that ye are thereunto called, that ye should inherit a blessing" (1 Peter 3:9)

"Saints...shall inherit the kingdom of God" (2 Nephi 9:18)

We become "joint-heirs with Christ" (Romans 8:17)

"Thou hast...given unto me a right to thy throne, and not of myself" (Moses 7:59)

"I will be merciful unto you, for I have given unto you the kingdom." (Doctrine and Covenants 64:4)

"For ye are lawful heirs" (Doctrine and Covenants 86:9)

"For even yet the kingdom is yours" (D&C 82:24)

"And if ye be Christ's, then are ye Abraham's seed, and heirs according to the promise" (Gal. 3:29)

"They shall inherit eternal life" (Doctrine and Covenants 50:5)

We shall "be partakers of the inheritance of the saints" (Colossians 1:12)

"The kingdom [God's estate] is yours and the blessings thereof are yours, and the riches of eternity are yours" (Doctrine and Covenants 78:18)

"The meek shall inherit the earth" (Matthew 5:5; see also Alma 5:51, 58; Alma 40:26; 3 Nephi 11:38)

The majestic miracle of salvation and exaltation is that we already have been promised unfathomable rewards. Remember, bequests from someone's estate are established in writing beforehand and the beneficiaries are usually aware of the future gift that will be transferred out of the estate at some future date. Our decision becomes whether or not we will retain the rights to our inheritance. The issue is not whether we are ever going to do enough to "earn" eternal life—that has already been done by Jesus Christ. Elder Boyd K. Packer offered instructive commentary:

> Some worry endlessly over missions that were missed, or marriages that did not turn out, or babies that did not arrive, or children that seem lost, or dreams unfulfilled, or because age limits what they can do. I do not think it pleases the Lord when we worry because we think we can never do enough, or that what we do is never good enough.[7]

We should be developing an intense desire to *retain* what we have—the promise of an inheritance of glory in the kingdom of our Father. Salvation in any form is not something we earn—it is a bequest that has already been given to us. Although material bequests transferred to heirs consist of differing assets (cash, CDs, savings bonds, stocks, real estate, and so on), the composition our heavenly bequests differ as Elder Packer pointed out, the eternal assets we receive will be priceless. The only issue to decide is if we will retain the rights to this precious gift and endowment. Unlike here in mortality where we cannot spend our earthly inheritance BEFORE it is transferred to us, we can forfeit the rights to our inheritance by choosing NOT to continue moving forward on the "covenant path." From experiences in my professional career, there is almost nothing as sad or tragic to witness people needlessly and frivolously "waste" their inheritance. It is infinitely more important that we retain the inheritance we have been given because of the atoning sacrifice of Jesus Christ.

Pray for Proper Desires

James E. Talmage wrote,

> Prayer is not compounded of words, words that may fail to express what one DESIRES to say, words that so often cloak inconsistencies, words that may have no deeper source than the physical organs of speech, words that may be spoken to impress mortal ears... prayer is made up of heart throbs and the righteous yearnings of the soul, of supplication based on the realization of need, of contrition and PURE DESIRE... if there lives a man who has never really prayed, that man is a being apart from the order of the divine in human nature, a stranger in the family of God's children. Prayer is for the uplifting of the suppliant. God without our prayers would be God; but we without prayer cannot be admitted to the kingdom of God. So did Christ instruct: "Your Father knoweth what things ye have need of, before ye ask him."[8]

A loving, kind Heavenly Father is in charge of our curriculum. He has a uniquely tailored plan to educate our desires. Our responsibility is to discover it, not change it. We may not be fond of our classroom tutorials nor the homework assignments. But they are the best tutorials for our growth and development as we sojourn here in our earthly laboratory, learning how to think and act like God. President Joseph F. Smith wrote,

> The education of our desires is one of far-reaching importance to our happiness in life; and when we learn that there is an education for our intellects and we are set about that education with prudence and wisdom, we shall do much to increase not only our happiness but also our usefulness to the world. *God's ways of educating our desires are, of course, always the most perfect.... and what is God's way?* Everywhere in nature we are taught the lessons of patience and waiting.[9]

One would be hard pressed to define a happier or more peaceful state of mind than to know that we are pursuing a course in life that is in accordance with the will of God.[10] Elder Robert D. Hales assured us, "Revelation [removal of doubt and uncertainty] comes on the Lord's timetable, which often means we must move forward in faith, even though we haven't received all the answers we desire."[11] Educating our desires is a *process*, not an *event*. It is part of the restorative process associated with the continuing restoration of the gospel in the dispensation of the fulness of time. Just as the Lord instructed Joseph how to conduct temple ordinances, there is order to the process. We proceed in an orderly manner (see Doctrine and Covenants 88:119).

Desire to Doubt Your Doubts

While Jesus and the three chief apostles, Peter, James, and John, were experiencing the magnificent events that occurred on the Mount of Transfiguration (including the reception of vital keys of the priesthood from ancient prophets who held them), a desperate father brought his son who had a "dumb spirit" (Mark 9:17) to the remaining nine apostles. He pleaded with them to cast out the evil spirit. Even though this was a righteous desire of both the boy's father and the nine apostles, the desired outcome was not achieved. Upon seeing Jesus, having descended from the Mount of Transfiguration, the father compassionately sought again for a blessing to bring relief for his son. In response to the Savior's statement, "If thou canst believe… straightway, the father of the child cried out, and said with tears, Lord, I believe; help thou my unbelief" (Mark 9:23–24). The New International Version renders this passage as follows, "Help me overcome my unbelief." It has always impressed me that Jesus did not condemn the father for having doubts; rather, He granted the distraught father's sincere desire. When we, like the grieving father confess our weakness to Him who has all power, we open ourselves to the Master's strength. Our souls then acquire conviction that defies doubt and replaces it with faith. We remember the words of the hymn "When Faith Endures":

I will not doubt; I will not fear; God's love and strength are always near.

His promised gift helps me find an inner strength and peace of mind.[12]

Alister McGrath wrote,

Doubt is a perennial problem in the life of faith. Doubt reflects our inability [without divine input] to be absolutely certain about what we believe. As Paul reminds us, we walk by faith, not by sight (2 Corinthians 5:7), which has the inevitable result that we cannot prove every aspect of our faith. This should not disturb us too much…the simple fact is that everything worth believing goes beyond what we can be absolutely sure about.[13]

Doubt has a major role in the eternal principle that "there is an opposition in all things" (2 Nephi 2:11). Doubt and faith are in total opposition. Doubt undermines the faith needed to sustain our righteous desires until they are fulfilled in accordance with the Lord's timetable. Alistar McGrath also wrote,

> Doubt reflects the continued presence and power of [un-repented] sin [transgression] within us, reminding us of our need for grace...our limitations as God's fallen and fallible creatures prevent us from seeing things as clearly as we would like.[14]

Another objective connected to doubting our doubts when educating our desires is described succinctly by Cyprian, bishop of Carthage, and an avid defender of the faith during the post-apostolic era: "Into my heart, purified of all sin, there entered a light which came from on high and then suddenly, and in a marvelous manner, I saw certainty succeed doubt."[15] Nephi, who "having great desires to know of the mysteries of God [which I would submit reflected his desires to remove doubts from his mind about the words of his father concerning, among other things, the need to leave Jerusalem] cried unto the Lord;...and he did visit me, and did soften my heart that I did believe all the words which had been spoken by my father" (1 Nephi 2:16).

A recent phenomenon, which in one sense could be described as "fiery darts of the adversary" (see 1 Nephi 15:24; Doctrine and Covenants 3:8, 27:17) being incessantly showered upon us from destructive cannons of the Internet, initiated publication of essays by the Church on a number of topics that address subjects such as the Women and the Priesthood, and Same-Gender Marriage, and so on. Given the potential risks of having faith being damaged and perhaps abandoned by some members of the Church, the Brethren have determined that clarifying and declarative statements of the Church's position are the best antidotes to the erosive effects of doubt and unbelief. Such statements are also "booster shots" to bolster the faithful by providing additional and more in depth understandings wherein they could hang their proverbial hats. It is interesting that a similar scenario previously occurred in the Church. In 1865, the First Presidency counseled the Latter-Day Saints:

> We do not wish incorrect and unsound doctrines to be handed down to posterity under the sanction of great names, to be received and valued by future generations as authentic and reliable, creating labor and difficulties for our successors to perform and contend with, which we ought not to transmit to them. The interests of posterity are, to a certain extent, in our hands. Errors in history and in doctrine, if left uncorrected by us who are conversant with the events, and who are in a position to judge the truth or falsity of the doctrines, would go to our children as though we had sanctioned and endorsed them....we know

what sanctity there is always attached to the writings of men who have passed away, especially to the writings of the apostles, when none of their contemporaries are left, and we, therefore, feel the necessity of being watchful upon these points.[16]

We escape the realm of the unknown (aka our doubts) not by lingering in the mire of doubt nor continuing to wander in the darkness, scorn, and ridicule scattered by the winds of hot and blustery words emanating from those residing in the great and spacious building, but rather by delighting in and expanding our knowledge of that which God has already revealed. Serious and consistent studying, along with pondering and prayerful consideration of institutional revelations, i.e., the standard works and the words of living prophets and apostles, result in individual revelations that dispel the mists of doubt and confusion. Willfully suspending our doubts and devoting our efforts to coming to a greater understanding of what we do know is a viable strategy to implement when we find ourselves buffeted with doubts and dodging those pesky "fiery darts" of the adversary.

We should keep in mind several other perspectives as we consider our doubts. (1) Not everything has been revealed. (2) I have not paid a sufficient price to resolve the issue. (3) I could be looking in the wrong places. (4) There are other things I need to learn first in order to understand the resolution to my doubts. (5) I am not God, who knows all things. Last, we will remain on the covenant path if we remember what Elder Jeffrey R. Holland said, "What we know trumps what we don't know."[17]

Desire to Receive the Joy of Repentance

When the Lord revealed that the New Jerusalem and temple were to be built in Missouri, He also said that the "gospel is the gospel of repentance" (Doctrine and Covenants 84:27). When we remember that the word gospel means "good news," the principle of repentance is illuminated in an unmistakable positive light. Some, however, mistakenly view repentance as punishment that must be endured for sins, transgressions, and mistakes. Others have incorrectly concluded that repentance is simply to stop doing things that are wrong. Furthermore, many have come to believe that repentance is a recipe or checklist—follow the formula and magically sins will be forgiven. Such notions are the exact opposite of the truth. The Apostle Paul taught, "We have not followed cunningly devised fables" (2 Peter 1:16). Repentance is among our greatest blessings.

In launching the Restoration, the Lord explained to the first missionaries that "the thing which will be of the most worth unto [them and us] will be to declare repentance" (D&C 16:6) Why? So that they might desire the joy of repenting!

The following experience was related to me by a friend and former bishop. He recounted that while making his way through the hallway toward the chapel to begin sacrament meeting, a young woman from his ward stopped him and said,

> "Bishop, I really need to talk to you. It will take just a minute." Thinking her matter of concern would be some minor item, he stopped and listened. "Last night," she blurted out, "I was involved in a violation of the law of chastity." She said just enough more that he knew it was a serious violation of commandments and covenants. Before he could stop her and set up an appointment for a proper interview, she continued, "But it's OK, because I stayed up all night going through the steps of repentance. Confessing to you, as I now have, was the only one I had left on the checklist. So I think I am ready to partake of the sacrament."

That experience, which happens more than it should, illustrates a dangerous misunderstanding and cunningly devised fable that some members of the Church seem to have subscribed to concerning the true nature of repentance and forgiveness; namely, the notion that this vital process is an event and results from following a simple "repentance recipe" or "formula forgiveness" based on a checklist of a certain number of steps. Because repentance and forgiveness are the very essence of our eternal salvation, it should not be surprising that Satan tries very hard to foster all manner of false doctrine, misinformation, and incorrect attitudes regarding this essential process—cunningly designed fables, as it were.

Satan pushes the repentant sinner toward either end of a broad spectrum of ideas concerning repentance and forgiveness. At one extreme, he seeks to convince us that true repentance for all our sins and transgressions is just too hard, and that forgiveness is virtually unattainable, and that even if we do repent, all will be lost if we do not live perfectly thereafter. In other words, he tries mightily to discourage us from even trying to gain forgiveness. Too often, this strategy succeeds and many give up believing it is overwhelmingly difficult.

Equally false is Satan's argument on the other end of the spectrum. As illustrated by the misguided young woman in the incident above,

Satan tries to convince us that repentance is easy and that forgiveness is available just by going through a checklist of a few simple steps or following a "canned" recipe or formula. Pour in a few ingredients, stir vigorously, and repentance emerges. Listening to this philosophy mingled with scripture, confuses and misleads our desires with the consequence of not being forgiven and missing out on the joy that repentance is designed to bring into our lives.

We need to ask a basic question: What is it that brings about a remission of our sins, transgressions, and mistakes? Although many members of the Church believe they know the answer to that question, they often only know part of the answer, and that part is usually the least important. That least important portion of the answer is often couched in a popular teaching device called the "Rs of repentance." This method sees to define repentance process by using a list of words that begin with the letter R. Nearly every member of the Church, even the very young, has heard a number of talks and lessons employing this pedagogical device, and can most readily list at least two or three of these R words. Though some teachers and speakers enumerate as many as eight or ten Rs, the basic six on most lists are as follows:

1. RECOGNIZE the sin, transgression or mistake
2. REMORSE for the sin, transgression, or mistake
3. RESOLVE to change behavior
4. RELATE the incident to the proper priesthood leader when it is of a serious nature
5. Make RESTITUTION, as far as possible, to those who have been injured by the sin
6. REFRAIN from the sin, transgression, or mistake.

Other creative words are sometimes added to the list. For instance, when a class of seminary students was asked to come up with additional "R" words one young man volunteered, "Well, if the sin is really bad, you might need to RELOCATE." Unfortunately, pneumonic devices do not teach the whole truth or even the most important part of the truth about either repentance or forgiveness. This model may actually be an obstacle, doing more harm than good by leading some people to believe that the "R" checklist is a complete recipe for repentance and a full formula for forgiveness.

Repentance and forgiveness is centered in the Atonement of Jesus Christ. **REDEEMER** is the omitted and overlooked "R word" in the process. Without the Redeemer as the lynch pin of the process, all the other steps fail to achieve the desired forgiveness. Failure to recognize our complete dependence on the Savior in seeking repentance and receiving forgiveness is truly making a serious oversight. What a huge mistake to speak of the process of repentance and forgiveness as if it were somehow a "do-it-yourself" project. It smacks of Satan's pitch to the spirit children of God in the pre-earth life—"surely I will do it" (Moses 4:1). In contrast, Nephi writes, "We talk of Christ, we rejoice in Christ, we preach of Christ, we prophesy of Christ, and we write according to our prophecies [and why do we do these things?] "... *that our children may know to what source they may look for a remission of their sins.*" (2 Nephi 25:26, emphasis added) Only when we realize that the purpose of repentance is to be reconciled to God through the "sufferings and death of him who did no sin" (Doctrine and Covenants 45:4) do we truly begin to understand repentance and appreciate the blessing of forgiveness. Hence, we come to the conclusion that the "R words" on the list—used either individually or collectively—do not bring about a remission of sins but, at best, lead us to our Redeemer, who can alone can grant a forgiveness of sins (see Luke 5:21).

A second "R" word frequently over looked is **RIGHTEOUSNESS**, not just the righteousness of refraining from the sin, transgression, or mistake (and by the way, refraining is not complete repentance as some have incorrectly rationalized), but the type of righteousness we actively seek, namely "to establish his righteousness" (Doctrine and Covenants 1:16). It is the difference between having a testimony of Christ and being "valiant" in that testimony. Repentance and the ensuing forgiveness are freely extended to us through the grace of Christ's Atonement, but they are accepted and actualized by our righteousness, which flows from true faith in the Redeemer, the author of our salvation. Elder Bruce R. McConkie explained it this way:

> Repentance is complete only as we live pertaining to the things of the Spirit... we must first gain an attitude of righteousness—a desire to live righteously—to gain forgiveness. The repentance Christ requires is a lifelong endeavor rather than a "checklist" approach... Sanctification... is the process by which we become continually and progressively cleansed from every form of sin... It is a PROCESS. Nobody is sanctified in an instant, suddenly.[18]

Repentance takes sincere desire, including an overarching desire to regain closeness to God. Repentance is efficacious in renewing our souls, moving us upward and further away from fallen-ness, "relying alone upon the merits of Christ, who was the author and the finisher of their faith" (Moroni 6:4). We should cease measuring our effort and achievement of repentance in terms of it being an event. We should recognize that desiring to repent and become less fallen is and will continue to be an on-going process. Pace of progress is not always a significant barometer in determining if our repentance is acceptable to God. Direction is far more critical. The Hebrew word translated as repentance is *TESHUVAH*, which means "turning back to God." A different picture emerges which brings our desires into sharper focus by providing more clarity. Turning away from sin and transgression and pointing ourselves back toward the covenant path is repenting.   Being forgiven (justified) places us back on the covenant path to resume the process of sanctification.

Desire to Have a Teachable Heart

One theme found in Book of Mormon is receiving forgiveness. People who had genuinely softened their hearts and sincerely sought forgiveness through repentance received it. And they received it immediately, meaning they were placed on the covenant path with the loving invitation to move forward. The Mulekites pondered the "immediate goodness of God" (Mosiah 25:10) and their desires became flames brightly burning to lead themselves and others along that path. Amulek promised the humble (soft-hearted and teachable) Zoramites that "if ye will repent and harden not your hearts, immediately shall the great plan of redemption will be brought about unto you" (Alma 34:31). A soft heart is teachable, thus enabling the instruction of our desires.

We experience an expansion of our views of the meaning and purpose of mortal experiences. Our desires for the gospel's blessings to flow and reach the entire family of our Heavenly Father, both here on this earth and in the spirit world can hardly be restrained. Some mistakenly think that unless we are perfect (Matthew 7:48), God will not help us; and since we aren't perfect, then our position is hopeless. I believe what Jesus meant was "The only help I will give is to help you become perfect. You may want something less, but I will give you nothing less." A soft and teachable heart desires and receives such help.

Our State of Being—The Result of Educating Our Desires

Among many prophets who have shared with God's mortal children, glimpses of the events and circumstances surrounding Judgment Day are Alma the Younger, Joseph Smith, and President Dallin H. Oaks. They have consistently reiterated the notion that our eternal "state of being" rests on essential criteria:

- Our works
- Our intentions and desires

Over the course of human history, works has gotten its fair share of gospel exposition—whether it be oratory or the written word. When it comes to intentions and desires, there probably hasn't been as much dialogue. I should take the opportunity to mention that distinguishing between intentions and desires seems to be in the category of drawing lines of demarcation between belief and faith and knowledge; namely, when does belief become faith and when does faith become knowledge? Obviously, this goes beyond the scope and purpose of this book.

The context for Alma the Younger's formulation of the concept of "state of being" arises during his patriarchal counsel given to his sons Helaman and Shiblon. In recounting his conversion experience, Alma the Younger teaches his sons (and us) some magnificent truths about mortality and what matters most. The reader will recall the familiar scenario of the angelic intervention to cause Alma the Younger and his colleagues, the four sons of Mosiah, to finally perceive their "state of being" as natural, fallen men who had become voracious enemies of God and his earthly kingdom. Remember that Alma the Elder (a prophet) and King Mosiah had tried numerous times to cause their sons to recognize their state of being. Their numberless attempts fell on deaf ears and unresponsive hearts. Thus, an angel was sent with a specific assignment. President Wilford Woodruff counseled us, "If the Lord sends an angel to anyone, He sent an angel to perform a work that could only be performed by the administration of an angel."[19] Significantly, and perhaps most important to us, Alma the Younger and the sons of Mosiah came to understand that, by continuing to do what they had been doing to become what they had become, they would become even greater enemies of God and further and further away from what God desired them to become. So it is with each of us.

I recall a critical moment in my life about twenty years ago. It did not involve an angelic intervention, but rather a friend who was also one of my clients. Unsolicited, he made the following comment to me (which I know he did not realize was an intervention from Heavenly Father to me): "If you keep doing what you are doing, you will keep getting what you are getting." Pondering on this simple but profound gem, I perceived with greater clarity what I had become in my career, and that doing the same things over and over, was not going to change anything. It was reminiscent of the question, "What is insanity?" Answer equals doing the same things over and over and expecting a different result. And, even more scary was the thought that twenty or thirty years into the future, I would have become just an older (and probably dumber) version of what I currently was in the present day. Spurred by that insight, I opened my own CPA practice—a change that has made all the difference in my professional career.

Likewise, Alma the Younger and his brethren saw their current "state of being" as well as their future "state of being" at the end of that road. The angel then showed them an alternative of what their "state of being" could be if they availed themselves of Jesus Christ's Atonement, which was still one hundred years away. As a result, they made overt choices to change their works, intentions, and desires. Alma the Younger tells Helaman that his initial desire was "that I could be banished and become extinct both soul and body, that I might not be brought to stand in the presence of my God" (Alma 36:15). Alma's subsequent desire, after inviting the power of the Atonement to become operative in his life (pains gone, not harrowed up with guilt and memory of his sins) and seeing God upon his throne, was "my soul did long to be there" (Alma 36:22) and "that I might bring souls unto repentance... bring them to taste of the exceeding joy" (Alma 36:24).

Thankfully, most of us do not need the kind of angelic intervention sent to Alma the Younger, the four sons of Mosiah, and Paul. We "come to ourselves" as did the prodigal son (Luke 15:15–32) and see what we have become. Given that becoming is a function of desires as well as works, it seems of vital importance that we become actively involved in the process of educating our desires. A disciple is one who is learning to be like God and Christ. Learning to think, feel, desire, and act as they do. In other words, doing things differently from what uninspired philosophers have touted for years in trying to explain the purpose of mortality. I recall William Law's simple statement: "If you will stop and ask yourselves why you are not as pious as the primitive Christians were, your own heart will tell you, that it is neither through ignorance or inability, but purely because you never thoroughly intended it."[20]

Notes

1. Brigham Young, Journal of Discourses 6:170.
2. Neal A Maxwell, *That Ye May Believe* (Salt Lake City, Utah: Bookcraft, Inc. 1992), 112–113.
3. LDS Bible Dictionary—Prayer, 752.
4. Orson Pratt, "The Holy Spirit," in a Series of Pamphlets (1852), Orson Pratt: Writings of an Apostle [Salt Lake City: Mormon Heritage Publishers, 1976] 57; emphasis added.
5. Brigham Young, Journal of Discourses 8:124.
6. From an address given at the seminar for new mission presidents on June 25, 2013.
7. Boyd K. Packer, "The Least of These," *Ensign*, Nov. 2004
8. James E. Talmadge, *Jesus the Christ* (Covenant Communications, Inc., American Fork, UT, 2006), 226.
9. Gospel Doctrine (Salt Lake City: Deseret Book, 1939), 197–8; emphasis added.
10. See Lecture Sixth, The Law of Sacrifice. Lectures on Faith
11. Robert D Hales "Personal Revelation: The Teachings and Examples of the Prophets," *Ensign*, Nov. 2007.
12. *Hymns*, No. 128.
13. Alister McGrath, "Knowing Christ" (New York: Doubleday Galilee, 2002), 79.
14. "Doubting: Growing through the Uncertainties of Faith" (Downers Grove, Illinois: IVP Books, 2006), 133.
15. Cyprian, bishop of Carthage, cited in Harold B. Lee, "Stand Ye in Holy Places" (Salt Lake City: Deseret Book, 1974), 57.
16. Brigham Young, Heber C. Kimball, and Daniel H. Wells, in Messages of the First Presidency of the Church of Jesus Christ of Latter-day Saints; Edited by James R. Clark, 6 vols. (Salt Lake City; Bookcraft, Inc. 1965–75), 2:232.
17. Jeffrey R. Holland, "Lord, I Believe," *Ensign*, May 2013.
18. "Jesus Christ and Him Crucified," Devotional Speeches of the Year, Provo, UT: Brigham Young University Press, 1976, 399.

19. Wilford Woodruff, Collected Discourses, 1886–1898, ed. Brian Stuy, vol. 5 Wilford Woodruff, Oct. 19, 1896.

20. C. S. Lewis, *The Restored Gospel According to C. S. Lewis* (Bonneville Books: Springville, Utah, 1998), 21.

CHAPTER 4
Sources of Desires

"Our desires are truly our own and cannot be...implanted from outside by anybody—even God—without dishonoring our individual moral agency."

—Elder Neal A. Maxwell[1]

The Genesis of Our Desires

Desires are triggered in one of two places—our hearts or our heads. Both righteous and unrighteous desires can be generated in either. Alignment with God's desires can initially be done intellectually as we learn truths from reading scriptures or hearing sermons. That process can also begin in the heart as the Spirit conveys truth through feelings, long before we gain a rational framework of understanding to supplement and support what our head is telling us and drawing us to do. By way of reminder, I would suggest the following as a working definition of desire, which seems to best fit our purpose, and be most useful in the process of educating of our desires.

> Desires characterize our inner-most feelings thereby representing the distillation of our strongest motivations and which truly calls the cadence for our thoughts and consequently our deeds. Our desires control the tilt of our soul. They control our choices which control the consequences to be felt both in this life and in the life to come. Desires are not something, given our free agency, which can be developed within us against our will. Desires are a profound part of our

personality. They lie at the root of our being. Ultimately, we become the composite of our desires.[2]

These are daunting but important parameters to explore as we consider the source of our desires. Desires reside in our hearts since the source of choosing to act on our desires is also found there. No wonder the Lord has given us a heads-up in this regard: "Behold, the Lord requireth the heart and a willing mind" (Doctrine and Covenants 64:34). Quite frequently but unintentionally, the word willing is inserted in front of heart when we read this verse. However, notice that the Lord's expectation is our hearts must do a complete buy-in, not just a willing heart, with no questions asked or reservations allowed. It is interesting to ponder that God only wants a willing mind. Many of the Lord's commandments and instruction have been given to us without explanations. Our minds want to rationalize as a basis for accepting and engaging with the Lord's direction even though the "why" just wasn't included with the revelation. Hence, our minds being willing is sufficient. The Lord found it necessary, on more than one occasion, to warn Joseph and certain brethren about vain and foolish imaginations (desires) that are most frequently sourced in our heads (see Doctrine and Covenants 35:7; 63:15; 45:49; 128:48; 129:116 and 136:19). At times, the desires of the mind can derail or override the desires of our heart. This is not to say that ideas presented to or conjured up by the mind can't be the genesis of righteous desires. However, the heart is the "innermost center" of our soul (spirit and body). We can summarize three valuable concepts about the heart as being:

1. The center of bodily life and power. When the heart is strengthened, the whole body is strengthened.

2. The center of the emotional nature of man. It is the seat of love and hate; it understands, deliberates, reflects, and evaluates; it is the center of feelings and affections, experiencing joy, pain, ill will, dissatisfaction, anxiety, despair, fear, and reverence.

3. The center of moral life. Many degrees of spiritual growth reside in the heart. It is the dwelling place of either Christ or Satan; it can be broken or hard; it can be a treasure of either good or evil in thoughts, words, and deeds...it is the center of the entire man, the very origin of life's impulses.

Education is a holistic endeavor that involves the whole person, including our bodies, in a process of formation that aims our desires (heart);

primes our imagination (mind); and orients us to the divine. Desires flow from the heart, influencing virtually every action and behavior, our feelings and attitudes, our sense of right and wrong. The mind can easily waver when it receives new or conflicting information. But our heart is the core of who we are. It is not so easily swayed or confused. So to ask for our whole heart is to ask for that constant part of our being that controls so much of our core values and beliefs. Father asks only for a willing mind because He knows that we can't control every thought and imagination that enters our head. So he only asks us to be willing to try and focus our minds on Him and His purposes, even when the explanation as to why is only partially given or not at all, leaving us to walk by faith. No wonder God cannot accept anything less than a complete commitment from our hearts. Remember that Martin Harris had pure motives emanating from his heart when he repeatedly petitioned Joseph to take the manuscript to "experts" who supposedly would verify the translation. The only difficulty it was a foolish and vain imagination concocted in his mind and not in harmony with the Lord's plan to have the plates translated. Martin had reasoned that translation by a noted and respected scholar would provide the necessary credence to overcome perceived and anticipated barriers of non-acceptance and unbelief.

God only requires a *willing mind*. Logically, one might then ask, "Well, doesn't the mind have desires, also?" Answer, yes. Some of them become righteous and perhaps unrighteous desires in our hearts. For example, as we search the revealed words of God emanating from his servants both past and present; as we listen to general conference or speakers in sacrament meetings or stake conference sessions, and even in Sunday School, Priesthood, and Relief Society classes, our minds can identity and latch onto wonderful ideas, which, when properly nurtured and correlated with the heart, can develop into righteous desires that are transferred to and written on our hearts so we can act upon them accordingly in the Lord's due time. However, the mind can also be a garden of unrighteous desires, which are referred to in the scriptures as "vain imaginations." Clearly, there is not a bright line separating the heart from the mind. The mind and heart interact connectedly. Often it can be difficult to "flesh out" a decision with the seemingly competing voices of our heart and mind. It is helpful to remember that regardless of our culture, our level of education, or economic status, at the depth of all of us, are the same desires—to love, to be loved, and to be happy.

May I draw on a personal experience to illustrate the tension and struggle that occurs when sorting out and choosing between conflicting desires initiated by our hearts and heads? While serving as a bishop, I had numerous occasions to interview priesthood leaders in my ward regarding the well-being of the members of their respective quorums (high priests quorum, Seventies—at that time—and elders quorum). One such evening when these Personal Priesthood Interviews had been scheduled, the elders quorum president arrived at the appointed hour. He was a good man, faithful, and devout in many respects. I had known him for a number of years, including prior to my being called as the bishop. He no sooner settled in the chair beside my desk, when without pause or giving me the opportunity to engage in church-like small talk, he blurted out, "Bishop, I'm struggling with the consequences of being submerged in pornography to the point of total addiction."

I invited him to explain, which he did in a manner indicative of having rehearsed a "speech" outlining his rationalizations and vain imaginations concocted in his mind to assuage the guilt swelling in his heart. He confessed to me that initially the pornographic images seemed innocent and really did not pose a threat. But now, it was an obsession. I hasten to point out that this occurred when there was no internet, computers, smart phones, websites, and video streaming so prevalent in today's world transmitting this filthy, additive material. The tears and emotions poured out as evidence of the long and terrible battle that had raged between what his mind wanted and what his heart knew was right. He loved the Church; he loved serving in his capacity; but the guilt and dichotomy of harmonizing the desires of his heart and head had become totally overwhelming.

So I said something to the effect that I had a pill that would make the desire to engage in pornographic activities go away. I said that I would put that pill on my desk in front of him and then asked, "Would you take it?" I saw the turmoil in his soul as he weighed conflicting desires being shouted by head and heart. Finally, after what to him was prob-ably an eternity, he lifted his eyes to look into mine and said, "I'm not sure…but I don't think I want to take the pill." Sadly, as he got up and slowly approached the door to leave, I put my arm on his shoulder, offered encouragement, and indicated that I was willing to talk about this again with him, should he so desire. Shaking his head no, he slipped out of my office never to return.

Over the years, based on this and similar experiences in working with people as a leader, I reached the heartrending conclusion that *"WHY" is where people go when they don't want to change.* The heart can and often does trump the vain imaginations and follies of the mind, but not always. The mind seeks the answer to WHY, and attempts to establish credible and soul-satisfying rationalizations for unrighteous desires in the hope that the guilt, which inevitably arises in the heart, will be assuaged. Almost always this process results in failure. No wonder there has been and will continue to be a seeming flood of counsel from the Brethren and other Church leaders to be careful about what we allow to enter our mind's eye, be it trashy books; filthy videos, movies and internet postings; to the insidiousness of pornography in all its forms. Not finding satisfactory or peaceful answers, we fool ourselves and succumb to those unrighteous desires and become swallowed up in vain imaginations.

Another conclusion I came to understand is that sometimes we erroneously and unwisely decide (based on input from either our mind or our heart) not to trust God's will and timing. The tutoring of our desires has a unique and divinely crafted lesson plan, which includes topics being taught in appropriate sequence. Elder Richard G. Scott in his October 1989 General Conference address taught us the connection between our desires and answers to prayers:

> Sometimes answers to prayers are not recognized [or in some cases do not come] because we are too intent on wanting confirmation of our own desires [whether they arise in our hearts or minds]. We fail to see that the Lord would have us do something else...I confess that I don't know how to make a correct decision except where there is righteousness and trust in a Heavenly Father. The principles will simply not work [meaning the answers won't come] when agency is intentionally used at variance with the will [desires] of God.

Uncertainty, tension, and doubt occurred repeatedly in the lives of members who came to me for counsel and advice. One of the blessings that distilled on my soul as a "judge in Israel" (and thankfully, it came early on during the seven years of my service in that calling) was that more often than not when members wanted to talk with me, what they really wanted from me was not counsel to change or a call to repent. They wanted me to tell them that their desires were okay to pursue. Many more Saints than I would have hoped left my office muttering that the bishop had not helped them because I would not agree with and reinforce their desires, particularly when they were contrary to the teachings of the gospel. As a judge in Israel, through the gift of discernment, I was able to know that such desires were not righteous.

Prioritizing Desires

In a BYU Devotional Address, Elder F. Enzio Busche underscored the importance of becoming aware of a magnitude of defined or undefined desires, conscious or subconscious desires. "We have to learn to summon them to our awareness, to analyze them, and then align them into order according to God's priorities. Studying the scriptures leads us to understand the importance of assessing desires."[3] Desires are constantly in a state of flux. Every life action is the result of our desires. Hundreds of different desires are fighting for supremacy within us. The act of categorizing them is a painful but needful act to initiate. Continuing, Elder Busche counseled,

> When we are not organized or focused, we may [desire] things that are irrelevant or even hazardous not only to our physical well-being but our spiritual development. Some desires stem from legitimate needs of our physical body—such as the need for food, shelter and rest—but our physical body is mostly capable of reflecting a self-centered orientation of the foolishness of the flesh. But the real part of us, or the real me, the spirit child of God, on the other hand, is the author of righteous desires, of our hunger for salvation, and our longing to eventually become reunited with our heavenly family. When the Holy Ghost, including the Light of Christ, is able to penetrate our hearts, prompted by the enlightened testimony of truth, it will cause in us a state of awakening, an awakening of the real me, the child of God, so that we can learn to channel desire to focus on true needs.[4]

Our Heavenly Father knows better than we do what we need to become like Him and His Only Begotten Son. Divine instruction is both necessary and sufficient not just to fulfill our desires, but also to know which desires to fulfill. He is constantly attempting to communicate those needs with us through His Spirit. When we listen to and follow heavenly promptings, some of which may be uncomfortable and soul-stretching, that the Holy Ghost often whispers to us, our desires will begin to align with His desires.

Elder Orson Pratt wrote,

The Baptism of fire and the Holy Ghost cleanses more thoroughly by renewing the inner man, and by purifying affections, desires and thoughts which have long been habituated in the impure ways of sin. Without the aid of the Holy Ghost, a person… would have but very little power to change his mind [desires]… and to walk in newness of life… hence, it is infinitely important that affections and desires should be, in a measure, changed and renewed, so as to cause him to hate that which he before loved, and to love that which he before hated; to thus renew the mind [desires] of man is the work of the Holy Ghost.[5]

Elder Pratt's counsel emphasizes the importance of living our lives in such a manner so as to always "have his spirit to be with them (us)." (Sacrament Prayer) The Holy Ghost renews our commitment to righteous desires; purifies them from earthly dross which cloud clarity, and where necessary changes our desires. President Nelson echoes this same theme as he is teaching us to seek for and obtain through the Holy Ghost personal revelation. Nothing could be more pertinent than having the Lord reveal to us those understandings, which are necessary to educate our desires.

Elder Busche further taught that "there are only two elements which separate us from the Holy Spirit—[1] the lack of desire to repent and [2] the lack of desire to forgive."[6] The frequently mentioned concept of repentance in the scriptures is to provide initial and continuing motivation to fuel our desires to repent. For instance, we all know and have undoubtedly experienced how difficult it is to stop doing things that are wrong, which is a fundamental element of the repentance process. If sin and transgression weren't fun, no one would be tempted to do engage in them. But just not doing wrong things anymore is not all there is to repenting. Repenting is more of reconciling and aligning our desires, which will then change our behaviors.

Similarly, forgiveness is mission-critical to successful completion of the plan of happiness. We can say we forgive; we can think in our minds that we have forgiven; but the crux of the matter is forgiving in our heart. The Lord has instructed us, "I, the Lord, will forgive whom I will forgive, but of you it is required to forgive all men" (Doctrine and Covenants 64:10). One of the marvelous and fascinating transformations that happen when we use regularly and consistently utilize our power to forgive is that we lose the power to condemn. What an unexpected blessing! But as is the case with so many principles, there is an opposite side.

Namely, if we continue to condemn, we risk losing our power to forgive. What a curse!

Unconditional forgiveness is another way of accepting human diversity with unconditional love, as God does, He who is no respecter of persons (Acts 10:34; Doctrine and Covenants 1:35, 38:16). We cannot be partial in our forgiveness, cannot have respect of persons, without denying our fundamental nature as children of God or trying to deny the most fundamental claim that others, including God, have upon us. If we have respect of persons (meaning not forgiving all men), we injure ourselves, others, and God. All human beings must be alike to God (2 Nephi 26:33), with no respect of persons, for God to be God. This principle must be true and our desires must be aligned with it for the great plan of salvation and happiness to work for us—for us to develop faith unto repentance, and to activate the power of Christ's infinite Atonement in our lives and the lives of others. Joseph Smith beautifully summarized this concept in the Lectures on Faith:

> It is necessary that men should have the idea that [God] is no respecter of persons, but that in every nation he that fears God and works righteousness is accepted of him, for with the idea of all the other excellencies of His character, and this one wanting, men could not exercise faith in him; because if He were a respecter of persons, they could not tell what their privileges were, nor how far they were authorized to exercise their faith in Him, or whether they were authorized to do it at all...but no sooner are the minds of men made acquainted with the truth of this point, that He is no respecter of persons, than they see they have the authority by faith to lay hold on eternal life, the richest boon in heaven, because God is no respecter of persons.[7]

Recognizing and prioritizing our desires also requires introspection. We need sacred time (Sabbath) and sometimes sacred space (temples) to enable our hearts to listen to the influence of the Spirit. It has been repeatedly taught that most inspiration comes as feelings. Such feelings can go unnoticed if we don't place ourselves where we can enjoy peace and quiet. I once read about a group of tourists on safari in Africa. They had hired several native porters to carry their supplies while they trekked through the jungle. After three days, the porters told the tourists that they would have to stop and rest for a day. They were not tired, they explained, but "we have walked too far and too fast and now we must wait for our souls to catch up to us."

We too can become so busy with the "cares of the world" (Doctrine and Covenants 39:9) and even perhaps the "busy-ness" of ministering that we neglect to replenish our souls. God himself was the first to replenish his soul after six days of labor on the Sabbath. "In six days the Lord made heaven and earth, and on the seventh day He rested and was refreshed." (Exodus 31:13) In Hebrew, the verbs translated as God's resting and being refreshed are shavat, which means "He Stopped" (from which we get the word "Sabbath;") and yinafash, which literally translates as "He got His soul back." (Sometimes, so much is lost in translation).

I don't think it is any accident or some form of coincidence that the Brethren have recently been emphasizing the Sabbath Day. What better way to check our bearings and fine-tune our focus to properly align the desires of our hearts and minds so that we might "get our souls back." Appropriate Sabbath worship enables us to off-load distractions and mis-understandings surrounding our desires to accomplish what President George Albert Smith once declared: "It is your duty first of all to learn what the Lord wants [desires]."[8] And therefore, concluded Elder Neal A. Maxwell, "Only by educating and training our desires can they become our allies instead of our enemies!"[9]

Desire Constancy and Consistency While Being Tutored

I recall conducting a session one Saturday afternoon in the Dallas Texas Temple. No sooner had we started than the rumblings of a summer's day thunderstorm could be heard. Several minutes went by until there was a particularly loud clap of thunder followed by the sound of a nearby power transformer exploding. The lights flickered and went out. We sat in darkness for what seemed like many minutes, but momentarily, the battery-powered emergency light above the door to the ordinance room came on. I stood and assured the patrons in the session that all would be okay; I asked them to remain calm, to refrain from communicating, and that we would soon receive instructions from the temple presidency as to what we should do and how to proceed.

As the anxious moments passed, I could see the countenance of a few patrons change from having a desire to be in an endowment session to wanting to leave. After about thirty minutes, several of the patrons left. It seemed to be an ill-advised decision given that they had no knowledge of what the circumstances were outside of the temple—for instance, downed power lines, traffic signals not functioning, flooded streets, cars that had perhaps collided or skidded off the slick streets, and so on. I wondered why they would leave the safety of the temple and became dismayed at how quickly the level of their desire to serve had waned. Not long after the patrons who had decided to go out into the storm left, the power was restored and the session was completed without further incident. It is not my intent to judge those who decided to leave, just merely to emphasize that we should remain committed to our desires and resulting choices. Blessings come to those who persevere while holding onto their righteous desires.

In sum, to make the proper choice on any issue is of far more importance to us personally than is the immediate outcome of the issue upon which we make a decision. The choices we make will affect the scope of our agency in the future. What we will have tomorrow depends on how we decide today. It is heartening to know that God's desires are a sure foundation and that if our desires are in line with His, then we do not need to worry about our choices being mistakes.

A quote from Joseph Smith continues to leave an indelible imprint on my soul. After being released from Liberty Jail in Missouri, Joseph returned to Nauvoo. Brothers Daniel Tyler and Issac Behunin called at his home and engaged in lively conversations on several subjects, primarily the persecutions endured by the Prophet. Joseph described how brutally he had been treated and laid the blame on false brethren who had apostatized from the Church. Brother Behunin then remarked, "If I should leave this Church, I would not do as those men have done; I would go to some remote place where Mormonism had never been heard of, settle down, and no one would ever learn that I know anything about it." The Great Seer immediately replied: "Brother Behunin, you don't know what you would do. No doubt these men once thought as you do. Before you joined this Church you stood on neutral ground. When the gospel was preached, good and evil were set before you. You could choose either or neither. There were two opposite masters inviting you to serve them. When you joined this Church you enlisted to serve God. When you did that, you left neutral ground, and you can never get back onto it."[10] Engaging and remaining committed to our righteous desires builds a fortress that will keep us from slipping back to what we could mistakenly think is neutral ground, when in reality it is the realm and home field of the great adversary. Not a good place to be.

Notes

1. Neal A. Maxwell, *The Education of Our Desires* (University of Utah Institute of Religion Devotional, 5 January 1983; transcribed by Daniel R. Mower).
2. Ibid.
3. "Understanding the Dormant Spirit," Brigham Young University 1995–96 Speeches.
4. Ibid.
5. Orson Pratt, "The Holy Spirit," in a Series of Pamphlets (1852), Orson Pratt: Writings of an Apostle (Salt Lake City: Mormon Heritage Publishers, 1976), 57.
6. "Understanding the Dormant Spirit," Brigham Young University 1995–96 Speeches; emphasis added.
7. Lectures on Faith, Third, para. 17.
8. George Albert Smith, 112th Annual Conference of the Church of Jesus Christ of Latter-day Saints, April 1942.
9. Neal A Maxwell, "According to the Desires of Our Hearts" *Ensign*, November 1996, 22.
10. Joseph Smith, "Recollections of the Prophet Joseph Smith" *Juvenile Instructor,* August 15, 1892, 491–92.

CHAPTER 5
Desire to Build Kingdom and Community

"Holy desires produce corresponding outward works"

—Brigham Young[1]

Desire to Defend the Kingdom of God

The next few chapters will delve into some specific desires that will arise once our desires are being educated and becoming aligned with God's. I don't attempt to recount and discuss every righteous desire, but some of those foundational desires upon which the gospel of Jesus Christ and the great plan of happiness is based. A desire to build and defend the Church is a fundamental component of the continuing Restoration of the gospel in the dispensation of the fulness of times. Certainly the courage to stand and defend the gospel and its divinely inspired earthly organization is founded in a righteous desire, which has been nurtured over the years by submitting our will to the will of God. Thus, the Church increasingly focuses on teaching the basics of the gospel, such as the great plan of happiness. Elder Jeffrey R. Holland explained the significance of the Church:

> This church, the great institutional body of Christ, is a marvelous work and a wonder not only because of what it does for the faithful but also because of what the faithful do for it. Your lives are at the very heart of that marvel. You are evidence of the wonder of it all.[2]

The Brethren are emphasizing the importance of staying on the covenant path—the path which we wanted to be on prior to coming to this fallen world. We promised our Heavenly Parents that we would share and teach the gospel, to reclaim those souls who wandered off the path. We understood that joining in the great and eternal work of God would work its greatness on us. Our desires need to be fully invested in the work. Neal A. Maxwell once counseled Church educators at BYU, "Do not underestimate the importance of what you do as articulators."[3] In praising C. S. Lewis, Austin Farrar wrote,

> Though argument does not create conviction, lack of it destroys belief… what no one shows the ability to defend is quickly abandoned. Rational argument does not create belief, but it maintains a climate in which belief may flourish.[4]

In defending the faith, you may also help another special group who needs particular strengthening. Lewis's mentor-in-absentia, George MacDonald, noted how "it is often incapacity for defending the faith they love which turns men [and women] into persecutors."[5]

Keeping ourselves and others on the covenant path today, more than ever, with the advent of so much secularism predicted not so long ago wherein traditional values are being challenged, good is being called evil and evil touted as good, absolutes are discarded for relativism in the name of enlightenment, defending the kingdom will be increasingly unpopular and ridiculed. Our desires to defend the kingdom will have to rise to the occasion, specifically now that President Nelson has asked us to not use any vernacular except "The Church of Jesus Christ of Latter-day Saint" when conversing or communicating in any manner about the name of the Church.

Desire to Hasten the Ongoing Restoration

Could there be a more fulfilling time than the dispensation of the fulness of times in which to live and witness firsthand the culmination of all that the prophets have seen and longed for over the generations? We are participating in the concluding episode of the earth's mortal existence before it will be born again by fire, and the promised millennial reign of Jesus Christ, King of Kings, will be ushered in and Satan and his influence will be cast out. Elder Neal A. Maxwell offered the following perspective on the "hastening of the work:

"For the Church, the scriptures suggest both an accelerated sifting and accelerated spiritual numerical growth—with all this preceding the time when the people of God will be "armed with righteousness" —not weapons—and when the Lord's glory will be poured out upon them. (See 1 Nephi 14:14; also 1 Peter 4:17; Doctrine and Covenants 112:25). The Lord is determined to have a tried, pure, and proven people (See Doctrine and Covenants 100:16; 101:4; 136:31] and "there is nothing that the Lord thy God shall take [desire] in his heart to do but what he will do it." (Abraham 3:17).[6]

As President Thomas S. Monson counseled, we must "ponder the path of our feet."[7] Church members have a special rendezvous to keep. Our dispensation is the focal point of all that has transpired in the history of this world. This is the season of restitution, and these are the days of restoration. God's children from over the earth are seeking the path that conducts them to the mountains (temples) and learning of his ways that they might continue to walk in His path. They want to find the tree laden with fruit to enable each of us to live after the manner of happiness and thus enrich the Church and our communities and nations.

Desire to Receive "the Greater Portion of the Word" (Alma 12:10)

Closely aligned with the desire to continue as willing participants in the ongoing restoration of the gospel is the desire to not become "hard in our hearts" as were Laman and Lemuel (see 1 Nephi 15:2–11). President Dallin H. Oaks warned,

If we harden our hearts, reject continuing revelation [from the Lord's anointed servants], and limit our learning to what we can obtain by study and reason on the precise language of the present canon of scriptures, our understanding will be limited to what Alma called "the lesser portion of the word."[8]

Among other things, the Ninth Article of Faith states, "We believe that He will *yet reveal many* great and important things pertaining to the Kingdom of God." Consequently, things *will* change insofar as they pertain to policies and procedures. For example, the recent changes regarding home and visiting teaching, and the combination of elders quorums and high priests groups. We should be open and receptive to all adjustments pertaining to the kingdom of God on the earth (the Church). Given recent events, we should be desirous of and anticipating further refinements in the future. What we have is not all that we will eventually have. A word of caution seems appropriate. It is not our responsibility to suggest to the Brethren or the Lord what we desire to change with regard to the kingdom of God and its operation here in mortality. The Lord will direct necessary adjustments and refinements. Our desires should be that we will see God's hand in all things; and, in response to earnest prayer, realize that God is in control, and that we will begin to see how the changes fit together.

Desire "to Hear the Music"

In his April 2015 General Conference address, Elder Wilford W. Andersen of the Seventy shared a delightful story where a young doctor found himself staring at an elderly Native American man who had shuffled into a hospital's emergency room. After couple of well-meaning inquiries to ascertain the nature of the man's malady, the doctor was taken aback when the Native American responded with "Do you dance?" After a few moments of bewilderment, the young doctor realized that the gentlemanly person standing before him was probably a medicine man. The doctor, thinking that he would obtain the desired information if he went along with the question asked of him, replied, "No, I don't dance...could you teach me to dance?" The old man's response caused Elder Andersen much reflection, as it should for us. "I can teach you to dance, but you have to hear the music." Elder Andersen then taught the gospel application,

> We learn the dance steps in our minds, but we hear the music with our hearts. The dance steps of the gospel are the things we do; the music of the gospel is the joyful feeling that comes from the Holy Ghost. It brings a change of heart and *is the source of all righteous desires*. The dance steps require discipline, but the joy of the dance will experience only when we come to hear the music. (emphasis added)[9]

The gospel equivalent of "hearing the music" is, of course, being converted. Conversion presents challenges to believers (both in the Church and out) to define, describe, or even characterize because it is so multifaceted. It is certainly not synonymous with membership or activity in the Church. We recall that Peter, who in spite of having "danced the dance" for more than two years with the Savior, was lovingly instructed by Jesus on the night before the crucifixion, "And when thou are converted, strengthen thy brethren" (Luke 22:32). In other words, hear the music.

The prophet-leader Nephi tried to create an understanding of being converted (hearing the music) in his final sermon to his people by outlining what arguably is a cogent description of how to hear music. "After ye have gotten into this strait and narrow path [i.e. dancing the dance], I would ask if all is done? Behold, I say unto you, Nay" (2 Nephi 31:19). Nephi continues by outlining how to hear the music, "For ye have not come thus far save it by the word of Christ with unshaken faith in him, relying wholly upon the merits of him who is might to save. Wherefore, ye must press forward with steadfastness in Christ, having a perfect brightness of hope, and a love of God and of all men. Wherefore, ... ye shall press forward, feasting upon the word of Christ and endure to the end." (2 Nephi 31:19–20)

As with several gospel principles, conversion (hearing the music) is not a "time-slotted" event; rather it is a continuing process—the ultimate goal of which is the perfecting of the Saints and preparing all things for the establishment of Zion. If we can't hear the music or are out of sync with the music, we need to re-align our desires. Both desires—not limiting ourselves to the lesser part and hearing the music—can be translated as meaning to "stay on the covenant path." A vital component of traversing the covenant path (which is a continuation of the path which we entered onto in the premortal existence) is to have the Holy Ghost as a constant companion and guide.

President Russell M. Nelson in his April 2018 General Conference address gave sobering prophecy: "In the coming days, it will not be possible to survive spiritually without the guiding, directing, comforting, and constant influence of the Holy Ghost." Then quoting President Lorenzo Snow, he said, "This is the grand privilege of every Latter-day Saint…that it is our right to have the manifestations of the Spirit every day of our lives." Finally he said, "Grow into the principle of revelation."[10]

The burning question which should be in every Latter-day Saint's mind is "Survive what?" I have pondered this question and have felt prompted that the "what" consists of several dangers. For example, I believe that the philosophies of men are going to be harder to untangle from scripture. I think the line between good and evil is going to become more blurred, making it nearly indistinguishable. I am sure that cultural trends both in and out of the Church will continue to diverge more and more from the will of God. Attempts will be made to overlay the "causes of the world" (aka social justice issues) that plagued James Covill (see

Doctrine and Covenants 39) and will be manifest by those wanting cultural changes to be made to the gospel. The only sure posture that will enable us to survive is the safety and assurance that comes with "increasing our spiritual capacity to receive revelation. We need to be more conversant with the language and messages of the Holy Ghost.

Desire "to Not Cast Away Your Confidence"

Paul's epistle to the Hebrews was written to the Jewish members of the Church living in Jerusalem. Paul returned from his third mission gratified to find that many thousands of Jewish members of the Church were still "zealous in the law" of Moses (Acts 21:20). It had been ten years since the conference held at Jerusalem wherein the apostles determined that certain ordinances of the law of Moses were not necessary for the salvation of gentile Christian converts, but that had not settled the matter for Jewish Christians. Paul wrote this epistle to show them why it was no longer necessary practice the ceremonies and rites of Judaism. His love for them is so wonderfully depicted as he encouraged them to, "Cast not away therefore your confidence, which hath great recompense of reward" [Hebrews 10:35]. He wanted them to hold onto the principles of the gospel, which they had embraced. The application of his timeless message is clear today—we should cast not away our confidence in the restored gospel, or abandon its inspired vehicle (the Church) to carry the message of salvation to the world, and in the appointed servants and friends of God, who direct the kingdom of God on earth. If such is the sincere desire of our heart, then truly there is great recompense of reward. Elder Jeffrey R. Holland spoke to buoy the Saints,

> I wish to encourage every one of you today regarding opposition that so often comes AFTER enlightened decisions has been made, AFTER moments of revelation and conviction have given us a peace and assurance we thought we would never lose…That is the way it has always been, Paul said, but don't "draw back" he warned. Don't panic and retreat. Don't lose your confidence. Don't forget how you once felt. Don't distrust the experience you had. That tenacity is what saved Moses when the adversary confronted him, and it is what will save you.[11]

With prophetic foresight of doubt and questioning that are plaguing some members of the Church two thousand years later, Paul counseled, "Call to remembrance the former days, in which, after ye were illuminated, ye endured a great fight of afflictions" [Hebrews 10:32]. Why would we believe that once we embrace the gospel that Satan would stop his war against God's plan in our lives? In particular, he continues his war of words to deflect or derail our desires from those that we chose in pre-earth life. Opposition, in its vast array of disguises, turns up almost everywhere that the good news of the gospel seed has been planted and begins to grow. We are not to cast away our confidence even when the storms of questions, doubts, and uncertainty blow seemingly in relentless waves against the institution, practices, policies, procedures, and even the integrity of current and former leaders of the Church. There will always be detractors and defectors who just can't leave the Church alone. Stand confidently with the combination of faith and knowledge you possess, for soon the sea will be calmed and the Prince of Peace will reign on this earth.

Desire to Bring Honor to Our Callings

There are many ways to serve and be involved in the kingdom. Each of us has and will have different callings. When President Harold B. Lee was a stake president, he approached a brother who had previously served as the first counselor in the stake presidency. Knowing that perhaps this good man might have some misgivings about being called to an assignment that was not as seemingly important as being a counselor in the stake presidency, President Lee asked if there were any concerns. The good brother responded, "We do not accept and serve in callings so that honor will be bestowed on us; we accept and serve in order to bring honor to whatever our calling is."[12] It is not about what our calling in the kingdom is, it is about how we serve while being in that stewardship. Are we making a difference in helping others to live the gospel and keep their covenants that are the guardrails along the straight and narrow covenant path to the tree of life?

Desire to Be of One Heart

We are familiar with the overriding purpose of this the dispensation of the fulness of times; namely, the establishment of Zion that will receive the Lord Jesus Christ as he ushers in His Millennial reign. One of the characteristics of that society is that "the Lord called his people Zion, because they were of one heart" (Moses 7:18). There is an interesting footnote reference for the words "one heart." The reader is pointed to 2 Chronicles 30. It would seem a bit unusual to be talking about Zion in this section of the Old Testament. A closer examination reveals that King Hezekiah of the Southern Kingdom in Judah desired that all of Israel, both the Northern and Southern Kingdoms should observe a solemn Passover in Jerusalem. Even though there was much tension between the Northern and Southern kingdoms, the invitation was extended to all twelve tribes of Israel to convene "a decree to make proclamation through-out all Israel, from Beer-sheba even to Dan, that they should come to keep the Passover of the Lord God of Israel at Jerusalem: for they had not done it of a long time in such sort [manner] as it was written" (2 Chronicles 30:5). All the children of Israel were invited to "be ye not stiff-necked, as your fathers were, but yield yourselves unto the Lord, and enter into the sanctuary" (vs. 8). "For the Lord your God is gracious and merciful, and will not turn aside his face from you, if ye return [repent] unto Him" (vs. 9). The proposal was not universally received initially. Several of the tribes laughed and mocked the king of Judah. But as the date grew closer, the naysayers humbled themselves (vs. 11) and came to Jerusalem. Now here is the key: Once all were gathered in Jerusalem, "the hand of God gave them one heart to do the commandment...by the word of the Lord" (vs. 12). Verses 13–25 outline the festivities of the seven-day ceremony, and then we come to verse 26: "So there was great joy in Jerusalem: for since the time of Solomon the son of David king of Israel [prior to the division between the northern and southern kingdoms] there was not the like in Jerusalem." The Lord created in them "one heart."

The relevancy of this remarkable re-uniting of the children of Israel as recounted in the Old Testament helps us today understand the need to overcome barriers, real and perceived, which have caused us to be sepa-rated from our brothers and sisters who are different culturally, ethnically, and so on than we are. Surely the Lord will help us create and build the bridges to connect us and feel a love that we didn't before. In addition, this story perfectly illustrates how a righteous desire, which in harmony with the will of God, can unite hearts in ways we might not have thought pos-sible. We can learn to love those who we don't really love yet. Establishing Zion can seem a bit overwhelming at times. And although the Saints in the early days of the Restoration were unsuccessful in accomplishing that goal, we can reject thoughts of dismissing our desires to build Zion because others failed. The saying goes that Rome wasn't built in a day. The Lord won't build Zion in a day, but He will show us how to put the pieces in place that form the infrastructure of that great society.

Desire to Extend Kindness

The starting point for unity lies in extending loving kindness to all who cross our daily path. Most people when asked would likely associate "Survival of the Fittest" with Charles Darwin. However, Darwin never wrote about survival of the fittest. Instead, his key theory is better characterized by "Survival of the Kindest." In what is known as Darwin's "sympathy hypothesis," he asserted that "those communities which included the greatest number of the most sympathetic members would flourish best and rear the greatest number of offspring."[13] Darwin didn't advocate brute strength as the primary indicator for a community's advancement; rather, he suggested that the key to societal longevity rested with how sympathetic, kind, and compassionate its members were. Without kindness and compassion, the survival and flourishing of our species would have been unlikely.

In the Torah, the Counting of the Omer marks the seven weeks between Passover—the physical redemption of the children of Israel from Egypt—and Shavuot—the spiritual redemption of the children of Israel when they received the Torah from God at Mount Sinai. The Omer counting serves as a narrative about each individual's journey from a place of constriction, toward a place of transformation. One virtue is assigned to each of the seven weeks; and, in stride with Darwin, the children of Israel deemed the most important virtue to be chesed—or compassionate kindness. To stress that notion even more pointedly, they assigned chesed to the first week of the seven-week process of Counting of the Omer.

Not long ago I read an article written by an admissions counselor at Dartmouth University (USA) where she recounted how seemingly small and unheralded acts of kindness had a profound impact on someone who wrote a letter of recommendation included in one of the many applications which crossed her desk annually.

> Every year I read over 2,000 college applications... the applicants are always intellectually curious and talented... But one quality is always irresistible in a candidate: KINDNESS. It's a trait that is hard to pinpoint on applications even if colleges asked the right questions. Every so often, though, it can't help but come shining through. The most surprising indication of kindness I've ever come across was the letter of recommendation for a student who had attended a large public high school in New England. This particular letter of recommendation caught my eye because it was from the high school's custodian.

This custodian wrote that he was compelled to support this student's candidacy because of his thoughtfulness. This young man was the only person in the high school who knew the names of every member of the janitorial staff. He turned off lights in empty rooms, consistently thanked the hallway monitor each morning and tidied up after his peers, even if nobody was watching. This student, the custodian wrote, had a refreshing respect for every person at the school, regardless of position, popularity, or clout.

Over 15 years and 30,000 applications in my admissions career, I had never seen a recommendation from a school custodian. It gave us a window onto a student's life in the moments when nothing "counted."[14]

When I read this article, I was reminded of something that J. R. R. Tolkien penned: "It is not our part to master all the tides of the world; it is to do what is in us for the succor of those years wherein we are set, *uprooting the evil in the fields that we know so that those who live after may have clean earth to till.*"[15] Such is ultimate loving kindness!

I read of Arturo Toscanini, the late, famous conductor of the New York Philharmonic Orchestra, who received a brief, crumpled letter from a lonely sheepherder in the remote, high mountain pastures of Wyoming. I can envision this easily, since I was born and grew up in Wyoming. The letter said, "Mr. Conductor, I have only two possessions—a radio and a old violin. The batteries in my radio are getting low and will soon die. My violin is so out of tune I can't use it. Please help me. Next Sunday when you begin your concert, sound a loud 'A' so I can tune my 'A' string; then I can tune the other strings. When my batteries are dead, I will have my violin." At the beginning of the ensuing Sunday's nationwide radio concert from Carnegie Hall, Toscanini announced: "For a dear friend and listener out somewhere in the mountains of Wyoming the orchestra will now sound an 'A'." The musicians joined in perfect unison together, sounding a perfect 'A.' The sheepherder only needed one note, just a little help to get his violin back into tune; he needed someone who cared to assist him with one string; after that, tuning the other strings would be easy.

There are so many desires connected to and embedded in efforts to build the kingdom. Some are glamorous and flashy; others are routine and seemingly dull. Regardless, the opportunities to educate our desires abound. We need to allow the Holy Ghost to guide us into doing what God wants, how He wants it done, and when He wants it done. Desires to build the kingdom of God are not measured by the size of the brick we add to the infrastructure already designed and in place.

Notes

1. Brigham Young, Journal of Discourses, 6:170.
2. Jeffrey R Holland, "Miracles of the Restoration," *Ensign*, Nov. 1994, 32.
3. Neal A. Maxwell, "Discipleship and Scholarship," Annual Banquet of the Foundation for Ancient Research and Mormon Studies, BYU, 27 September 1991. Published in BYU Studies, 32, No. 3, 1992, 59.
4. Austin Farrar, "Grete Clerk," in *Light on C. S. Lewis*, comp. Jocelyn Gibb (New York: Harcourt & Brace, 1965), 26.
5. George MacDonald, *Anthology* (New York: MacMillan, 1941), 121.
6. Neal A Maxwell, "For I Will Lead You Along," *Ensign*, May 1988.
7. Thomas S. Monson, "Ponder the Path of Thy Feet," *Ensign*, Nov. 2014, 86.
8. Dallin H. Oaks, "Scripture Reading and Revelation," *Ensign*, Jan. 1995, 7.
9. Neil L. Andersen, "The Music of the Gospel," *Ensign*, May 2015.
10. Russell M. Nelson, "Revelation for the Church, Revelation for Our Lives," *Ensign*, May 2018.
11. Jeffrey R Holland, "Cast Not Away Your Confidence," BYU Speeches 1999, 2 May 1999.
12. Harold B. Lee, "Be Loyal to the Royal Within You," BYU Speeches, September 11, 1973.
13. Charles Darwin, "Descent of Man" (John Murray, London, 1871), 72.
14 Rebecca Sabky, "Check This Box If You Are a Good Person," New York Times, April 4, 2017.
15. *The Return of the King*, The Lord of the Rings #3, J. R. R. Tolkien, (Ballantine Books, New York, 1955).

CHAPTER 6
Desires for
Personal Growth

"What we insistently desire, over time, is what we will eventually become and what we will receive in eternity."

—Elder Neal A. Maxwell[1]

President Brigham Young taught,

When the will, passions, and feelings of a person are perfectly submissive to God and His requirements, that person is sanctified. It is for my will to be swallowed up in the will of God (see Mosiah 15:7) that lead me into all good, and crown me ultimately with immortality and eternal lives.[2]

Consistent with Elder Maxwell's insight and President Young's counsel above, the overriding purpose of this mortal experience is to continue the process, which began in our premortal life, of aligning our desires with those of our Heavenly Father. We are in the perfect laboratory designed by a loving Heavenly Father to educate our desires where we undergo personal development in an environment where mistakes, missteps, errors, transgressions, and even sins can be erased and forward progress can be resumed. There are a number of desires that focus our efforts on personal development toward exaltation.

Desire the Spirit of Prophecy

At first glance, seeking to have a righteous desire for the spirit of prophecy may seem a bit presumptuous. After all, isn't this gift of the Spirit reserved for those called to prophesy—namely, the First Presidency; the Quorum of the Twelve Apostles; the Seventy; and to a lesser extent, stake presidents, and bishops. It would not seem necessary to recount examples and illustrations of the operation of this special gift in the history of the Church (a.k.a the kingdom of God on earth in its various forms over the centuries). However, many seem to not recognize that this gift has another dimension—one that is available to all members of the Church—which is the ability to read, understand, and properly interpret prophecies recorded in the scriptures, both ancient and modern.

Nephi wrote that those who were not "filled with the spirit of prophecy" (2 Nephi 25:1–4) could not understand the meanings of Isaiah's writings on the brass plates. Prophecy was, is, and always will be uttered under the influence and guidance of the Holy Ghost. Therefore, our desire should be to seek the promptings and guidance of the Holy Ghost who will teach us all things necessary to understand and properly interpret prophecies. This includes those pronounced by Isaiah, Jeremiah, and Ezekiel in the Old Testament, particularly those prophecies pertaining to the last days that are yet to be fulfilled and those recorded by John the Revelator in the Book of Revelation in the New Testament. Our desire should be to obtain the spirit of prophecy to assist us in that noble and worthwhile endeavor. One stimulus for this righteous desire is the counsel of Nephi, "For I know that [Isaiah's prophecies] shall be of great worth unto them in the last days" (2 Nephi 25:8). Therefore, sincerely seeking and developing the righteous desire to have the spirit of prophecy is not only appropriate, but necessary, and aligns one's desires with God's. As taught by Joseph Smith, we are never unworthy to pray and to ask for the spirit of prophecy as we study and ponder the scriptures.

Desire to Recognize "Spear-carriers"

While I was in high school, I participated in various dramatic arts productions. My junior year found me cast as Emily's father in *Our Town*, the classic play written by Thornton Wilder. Ironically, *Our Town* was part of the required reading in my American Literature class. In essence, I got a "double whammy" of the play. Even though I was young, inexperienced, lacking immaturity, and unseasoned, the play had an effect on me. So, several years later when I purchased a book of poetry written by Carol Lynn Pearson called *The Growing Season*, you would understand why I was so touched when I read her poem called "The Cast" which is based on the play, *Our Town*.

> I lost the starring part in Our Town to Linda, a girl not half as good as me, who kept her eyes down for the whole tryout, and even stuttered. When the cast was posted and the high school drama coach saw me reading it through my tears, he put an arm around me and said,
>
>> "Now, look—things are not always as they appear.
>> This is not Broadway, it's an educational institution.
>> We're here for two reasons—to put on a show,
>> But, more important, to help people grow. Someday you'll see."
>
> So Linda played Emily, and she didn't even stutter. And I was the Third Woman at the wedding watching and wondering how he knew what she could do if she had the chance. Since then I have guessed that God, being a whole lot smarter than my high school drama coach, might be offstage sometimes with an arm around a questioning cast:
>
>> "Now, don't try to outguess me. Sometimes the first shall be last and the last shall be first. And I have got my own reasons I need some strong ones to star and some strong ones to stand back. And I am going to put out front some you might not choose. But you will see what they can really do when they have the chance. We've got to put on the show, and, too, we've got to help people grow."
>
> As I walk through the scenes, watch the costumes move, and listen to the lines of the powerful, the weak, the rich, the poor; I look at leads with less awe than most, and at the spear-carriers with more.[3]

During my tenure as bishop of my ward, I had a number of experiences that taught me to view "spear-carriers" with more awe. For instance, there was the faithful young man who served as financial clerk during the first year of my calling. He helped me tremendously to successfully navigate the tithing settlement process. In those years, the Church's donation system was primitive in comparison to how it works today. It required a lot of manual recordkeeping, reports, and reconciling of donations. He did a magnificent job. You can imagine the panic that set in the following year when shortly before tithing settlements would begin, he announced that he had accepted employment resulting in greater financial compensation and growth opportunities—only it was in Salt Lake City, Utah (USA) instead of Dallas, Texas (USA).

I began to review the ward list with the hopes that inspiration would quickly come to identify the person that the Lord had prepared to serve in this significant behind-the-scenes, a.k.a "spear-carrier" calling. After three times through the list, including once with my counselors in a bishopric meeting, there had been no certainty forthcoming as to who was to be called. Driving home after that bishopric meeting, the Spirit whispered to me the name of a certain brother. My initial response was to reject the prompting. I thought, "This won't work for several reasons: he's recently moved into the ward, has not been a regular attender because his employment with the Federal government requires travel, and most significantly, his wife is not a member of the Church and is the daughter of a well-known Baptist preacher in the Texas Bible belt." I rationalized that she would probably not understand the time commitment involved. It was therefore reasonable that they might find their relationship strained with his service becoming a negative influence on their marriage. But the Spirit, ignoring my rational objections, whispered his name again, even louder the second time. I uttered a prayer of thanksgiving and told the Lord I would follow His inspired direction.

This good brother was called, accepted the assignment, and in many ways, turned out to magnify the calling in a manner equal to if not more so than the brother who had moved out of the ward. As I observed his diligent service, the words of "The Cast" came flowing to my mind, "You will see what people can do when they have the chance." From that time on until I was released, I frequently approached the process of identifying members for callings by putting the spear-carriers on the same level as the stars. But there was another blessing associated with this spiritual learning experience.

For a number of years, Paul Harvey, a news commentator, had a fifteen-minute nationally syndicated radio program known as, "The Rest of the Story," where he would relate little-known facts or circumstances about famous people, withholding their identity until the very last moment. This incident of my calling the financial clerk had a "Rest of the Story" component. About a year of his service in this assignment, I visited this good brother at his home to give him information from Sunday's donations. He had been out of town on a work assignment and was not in attendance at our Sunday meetings. While he was reviewing the paperwork that I had brought him, his wife pulled me aside and said, "I'm taking the missionary discussions and have decided to be baptized. Would you baptize me? And I want my husband to confirm me and bestow the gift of the Holy Ghost."

Truly, the Lord is a whole lot smarter than me (reminiscent of Isaiah's words—"For my thoughts are not your thoughts, neither are your ways not my ways, saith the Lord. For as the heavens are higher than the earth, so are my ways higher than your ways, and my thoughts than your thoughts" [Isaiah 55:8].) Heavenly Father had his reasons for calling this brother to serve. A short time later, I had the honor of baptizing her a member of the Church while her husband performed the confirmation. Initially, she was a spear-carrier, but when given opportunities to serve, all of us in the ward saw what she could do. Among other callings, she served both as a ward and stake Relief Society president. That's the "Rest of the Story." God bless the "spear-carriers" and educate our desires to see them with more awe.

Desire to Honor Gifts That We Think Less Honorable

Desires for spiritual gifts are regularly sought for among members of the Church, especially when viewed through the lens of the revelation given to the Prophet Joseph Smith on March 8, 1831 in Kirtland, Ohio, approximately one year after the organization of the church.

> That ye may not be deceived, *seek ye earnestly for the bests gifts*, always remembering for what [purpose] they are given... they are given for the benefit of those who love me and keep all my commandments, and him that seeketh so to do; that all may be benefited.... For all have not every gift given unto them; for there are many gifts, and to every man is given a gift by the Spirit of God... that all may be profited thereby. (Doctrine and Covenants 46:8–9, 11–12; emphasis added)

This revelation echoes what Paul taught 2,000 years ago in his first epistle to the Corinthians. After enumerating many of the same gifts of the spirit listed in Doctrine and Covenants 46, Paul then expressed an unusual insight that is not included in the revelation given to Joseph Smith.

> Nay, much more those members of the body [Paul had compared the various gifts to parts of the human body emphasizing the importance of each one], which seem to be more feeble, are necessary; and those members of the body which we think to be less honorable, upon these

we bestow more abundant honor; and our uncomely parts [gifts] have more abundant comeliness. (1 Corinthians 12:22–23)

Such doctrine was "foolishness to the Corinthian Greeks" who worshipped the perfections of the body. But Paul had a good reason for providing such wise counsel. From God's perspective we know he is not concerned with comparative, individual excellence of gifts but, rather, with helping all his children become like Him and guiding us as we learn how to use these special gifts that all might be benefitted. Here is Paul's reason:

> Our comely parts have no need: but God hath tempered the body together, having given more abundant honor to that part which lacked: that there should be no schism in the body; but that the members should have the same care one for another. And whether one member suffer, all members suffer with it; or one member be honored, all members rejoice with it. (1 Corinthians 12:24–26)

The "comely" gifts will get more than their share of attention in human society, so much so that Christ has to warn us to give them away, share them completely, or they will canker our souls and destroy as opposed to being a blessing to us and others. On the other hand, we must desire to see each other's gifts, however feeble and uncomely they appear in the world's eyes because our desires have deepened our understanding of the fatherhood of God and the brotherhood of man.

Recall the Savior's encounter with the man born blind. Consistent with the prevailing philosophy taught by the Hebrew scholars, his disciples asked, "Who did sin, this man, or his parents, that he was born blind? Jesus answered, "Neither hath this man sinned, nor his parents: but that the works of God should be made manifest in him" (John 9:2–3). We often do not believe and envision that our weaknesses and challenges are gifts that can bless others, but Christ showed us how they can be. In the process of desiring to see each other's gifts, whether comely or uncomely, God will open the eyes of our understanding to see the works of God made manifest.

I have a grandson Jack, who was born with significant physical and mental challenges. His father, my son-in-law, asked me for guidance as to what he should say when giving Jack his name and blessing. I suggested that what might be most appropriate is that each of us would see the hand of the Lord being manifest in Jack's life for the duration of his mission here on earth. (By the way, the only blessing pronounced was exactly that)

Jack is now five, and he is a happy, loving boy with a quality of life that no one expected. And the handiwork of God has surely been manifested.

In an address as president of the Association for Mormon Letters, Lavina Fielding Anderson related how she had learned, from a testimony at a gathering of Relief Society sisters in Nauvoo that these feeble gifts, even our weaknesses and vulnerabilities, are what we consecrate to the Lord in the temple to use as He will.

> Catherine Stokes, a black convert in a Chicago ward, related her experience of going to the temple for the first time. "I took my blackness with me and that was part of what I consecrated." Sister Stokes described how the sister temple worker, who assisted her through the initiatory ordinance, was barely able to articulate through her tears, and apologized at the end because she had not wanted her personal emotions to interfere with Catherine's experience. "I have never had the privilege of doing this for a black woman before," the temple worker explained, "and I'm so grateful." Sister Stokes reassured her, "That's all right. That's one of the things I can do for you that no one else in the temple today could do. My blackness is one of the [gifts] the Lord can use if He wants to—and apparently it has been a most successful collaboration."[4]

The twenty-third Psalm says, My cup runneth over." We should have the desire to see our lives as the accumulation of gifts (both comely and uncomely) that God has given us. Furthermore, once we have learned to appreciate what we have, as uncomely as those gifts may seem, we will cease to complain that we don't have more or different gifts (i.e. someone else's gift). Rather, we will seek "earnestly the best gifts, always remembering for what [purpose] they are given..." (Doctrine and Covenants 46:8) and come to see how to magnify and expand those gifts "that all may be benefited" (Doctrine and Covenants 46:9). The best thing we can do when we find out that our cup runs over with abundance from God's goodness is to get ourselves a bigger cup. Our ability to enjoy God's blessings is more a function of our capacity to receive them than of any limitations on God's ability to bless us. The more blessings we are capable of finding around us, the more we see and recognize that the "givens" in our life are gifts, the more God will bless us. No matter how large a bowl we set out to receive God's blessings, it will always overflow.

Another dimension of gifts is illuminated when precious gifts are temporarily taken from us. There is beautiful hymn titled "It is Well with My

Soul" written by Horatio G. Spafford (1828–1888) a Presbyterian laymen from Chicago. He was a devout Christian. He had an established and successful legal practice that garnered him a small fortune that evaporated in the wake of the great Chicago Fire of 1871. Having invested heavily in real estate along Lake Michigan's shoreline, he lost everything overnight. In a saga reminiscent of Job, his son died a short time before the financial disaster. But the worst was yet to come. Desiring a respite for his wife and four daughters, Spafford planned a European trip in 1873. In November of that year, due to unexpected last-minute business demands, he had to remain in Chicago, but sent his wife and four daughters on ahead as scheduled on the ill-fated S. S. Ville du Havre. He expected to follow in a few days. On November 22, the ship collided with the Lochearn, an English vessel, and sank in twelve minutes. The few survivors, which included Mrs. Spafford but not her four daughters, were eventually taken to Cardiff, Wales where she cabled her husband with the devastating news about the loss of their children. Spafford left immediately to join his wife. The following hymn was penned as his ship sailed through the area of the ocean where the ship carrying his four daughters had sunk.

> When peace, like a river, attendeth my way, when sorrows like sea billows roll; whatever my lot, Thou hast taught me to say, It is well. It is well with my soul.
> Refrain:
>> It is well with my soul; it is well, it is well with my soul.
>> Though Satan should buffet, though trials should come, let this blest assurance control, that Christ had regarded my helpless estate, and hath shed His own blood for my soul.
>> My sin—oh, the bliss of this glorious thought—my sin, not in part but the whole, is nailed to the cross, and I bear it no more, Praise the Lord, Praise the Lord, O my soul!
>> For me, be it Christ, be it Christ hence to live: If Jordan above me shall roll, no pang shall be mine, for in death as in life Thou wilt whisper Thy peace to my soul.
>> But, Lord, tis for Thee, for Thy coming we wait, the sky, not the grave is our goal; Oh, trump of the angel! Oh, voice of the Lord! Blessed hope! Blessed rest of my soul!
>> And Lord, hast the day when faith shall be sight, the clouds rolled back as a scroll; the trump shall resound, and the Lord descend, Even so, it is well with my soul.

Desire to Be Submissive

My experience has taught me that there are two levels of being submissive—first, submitting to our Redeemer, the Lord Jesus Christ. Undoubtedly, submission involves a submission to authority, but as Elder Neal A. Maxwell once said,

> Most forms of holding back are rooted in pride or are prompted by the mistaken notion that somehow we are diminished by submission to God. "In reality, the greater our submission, the greater our expansion.[5]

The second level of submission is to the Lord's servants. Leo Strauss, in his *Studies in Platonic Political Philosophies*, got it right when he declared that prophets give us unforeseen and unanticipated gifts when they tell us of truths which do not square with our reason or expectations. He said,

> True prophets, regardless of whether they predict doom or salvation, predict the unexpected, the humanly unforeseeable.[6]

These words remind us of Paul's admonition in teaching about the value of prophetic injunctions and counsel, "While we [meaning the prophets of God] look not at the things which are seen, but at the things which are *not seen*: for the things which are seen are temporal; but the things which are not seen are eternal" (2 Corinthians 4:18). How comforting it is to know that the Brethren are looking for and seeing things that are not seen; for example, consequences of adopting laws contrary to the laws of God (same-gender marriage comes to mind). With the passing of time in this the dispensation of the fullness of times, it is vital that we submit to the constant stream of messages being conveyed by the Brethren as they minister throughout the world.

In addition, like many other aspects of the gospel of Jesus Christ, submission is a process, not a one-time, singular event achieved through following a checklist or formula. The process of submission lifts us toward improvement and expansion of our minds and spirits. We know from our experience that we are changed for the better on those occasions when we submit to the authority of the Lord. On numerous occasions, we have humbly uttered, "Lord, what would you have me do?' thus forging our desires to be in accordance with God's desires through the revealed understanding to our souls distilling from the influence and gift of the Holy Ghost. Satan knows that this process works in both directions. He knows that all has he has to do is to whisper, or on occasion, yell, "Well, let's not be submissive for a while. Do what YOU want to do."

Submission also includes laying our will on the altar. In the end, it is the only thing that is completely ours and it is the ultimate sacrificial offering made using our moral agency. Submitting one's will to God's will is not always easy. The Savior himself declared, "I have suffered the will of the Father in all things from the beginning" (3 Nephi 11:11). Coming to Christ has a great deal to do with our willingness to "suffer the will of the Father." The implication is that submitting our will to God and aligning our desires with His will require sacrifice and likely some suffering.

Desire to Drink from "Deep Wells"

There is an interesting and frequently unnoticed symbol in the Old Testament narrative of Isaac, son of Abraham. It involves an insightful commentary about digging wells in Gerar.

> And Isaac dwelt in Gerar…; and the Philistines [who lived in that vicinity] envied him. For all the wells which his father's servants had digged years earlier, the Philistines had stopped them and filled them with earth… And Isaac digged again the wells of water, which they had digged in the days of Abraham his father; for the Philistines had stopped them after the death of Abraham: and he (Issac) called their names after the names by which his father had called them. And Isaac's servants digged in the valley, and found there a wells of springing [living] water. (Genesis 26:6, 14–19).

Like the parables taught by Jesus wherein many did not comprehend the deeper meaning of their symbolism, we have a similar situation here. For those who have been to the environs south and west of Beer-sheba, and from the Gaza Strip to the borders of Egypt as have I, you know that there is nothing (nada, zippo) there but rocks and sand. Water was and continues to this day to be a critical element of survival. Abraham had dug deep wells in a successful effort to find water that would sustain life. He prepared a map marking where these wells were so that Isaac would know where to find the precious liquid. Even though the Philistines had plugged Abraham's wells when he moved to another region, Isaac still knew where to dig. And he did re-open the wells to find life-sustaining water.

We find ourselves being warned by a prophet that we need to have living water to be able to survive—he has even given us a map of where to find the deep wells where flows the saving fluid; namely, the scriptures (particularly the Book of Mormon), the words of living prophets and apostles, and personal revelations received through the gift of the Holy Ghost. The obvious symbol from these few verses about digging wells in the desert is the water represents Jesus Christ. However, there is another profound symbolic lesson herein. The water found by Abraham and Isaac's servants also represents the will of God.

As discussed earlier in this chapter, righteous desires are centered deep in our hearts. They spring forth when aligned with God's desires and become the saving refreshment, which leads to survival in the spiritual desert. Modern Philistines may have filled our hearts with mortal debris, thus blocking access to the living water. We must be willing to remove all the accumulated trash in our hearts, which will then enable us to have access to and partake of the water. I further find it enlightening that drinking entails the activity of swallowing—"The will of the Son being swallowed up in the will of the Father" (Mosiah 15:7). Given this wonderful lesson about Abraham and Isaac digging wells, it seems critical that we desire to re-dig the wells in our heart and find deep in the recesses therein the living waters of God's will, and then let our wills and desires be swallowed up in His will.

Desire to Fill Our Souls with God-confidence

The Savior invited each of us to become perfect (i.e. finished and complete, which I hastily add will not be accomplished totally during our mortal probation). For many people this means that in order to be perfect, we need to have a healthy dose of self-confidence and self-esteem, which are good characteristics to have. . Worldly philosophers and self-improvement experts would have us believe that we need to increase our self –confidence in order to succeed in life by being our real self. However, having a desire to fill our souls with God-confidence would seem to be even more desirable. What is God-confidence? Ammon joyfully described "God-confidence" as being something far more desirable than self-esteem.

> I do not boast in my own strength, nor in my own wisdom; but behold, my joy is full, yea, my heart is brim with joy, and I will rejoice in my God. Yea, I know that I am nothing [same conclusion reached by Moses]; as to my strength, I am weak; therefore, I will not boast of myself, but I will boast of my God, for in his strength I can do all things. (Alma 26:11–12)

Ammon is teaching us that the whole concept of self-esteem is irrelevant. Being filled with God-confidence is of far greater worth than any sense of self-confidence. Knowing that one of the grand objectives of our mortal experience on this earth is to gain access to and fully accept the grace of Jesus Christ enables us to overcome our trials and be reconciled to God and His divine plan. We should immediately recognize that self-confidence is a puny substitute for God-confidence.

Among the glorious understandings that the Lord taught the Prophet Joseph in Liberty Jail was a correct notion about confidence in God. "Let thy bowels also be full of charity towards all men...let virtue garnish thy thoughts unceasingly; then shall thy confidence wax strong in the presence of God" (Doctrine and Covenants 121:45). The message for us is that love and virtue are essential ingredients in feelings of God-confidence. Isn't it possible that the pursuit of self-confidence actually diverts us from the connection God is trying to make? Might not self-confidence produce a false sense of "carnal security?" (2 Nephi 28:21) Without the guidance of the Holy Ghost, our pursuit of self-confidence could produce unnecessary levels of anxiety, uncertainty, doubt, pride, etc.

Some might disagree with the dichotomy being suggested between the pursuit of self-confidence and the acquisition of God-confidence. I believe it helpful to recall the words of the Prophet Joseph, "By proving contraries, truth is made manifest" (History of the Church, 6:428). For example, King Benjamin finds these two incompatible. He said to remember your own nothingness and God's goodness [Mosiah 4:5]. Would not attempting to have both be an acute manifestation of double-mindedness? James warned that a double-minded man is "unstable in all his ways" (James 1:8). So where is the need to pursue self-confidence? We don't need it. God-confidence will carry us further; in fact, it will take us to the end of the strait and narrow covenant path where stands the tree with the most precious and desirable fruit.

In many ways it appears that "self" may actually be an interloper in much of what we do and that we can only find relief from the stresses and strains of self-promotion by saying, in effect, "Get thee behind me, Self." President Ezra Taft Benson shed bright illumination on this concept, "Christ removed SELF as the force in his perfect life."[7]

Over the years, I have become acutely aware of how demanding of attention the "self" is. It has taken and will continue to take much prayer and focused, deliberate living for me to remove "self" as the force in my life. I have become painfully aware that most all of my transgressions rise out of the self-absorption of my heart, self-defense, and self-gratification. It appears clearly that a change is needed at the very fountain of my heart, out of which all desires arise. Could I actually arrive at a level where I would act without calculating my self-interest all the time? Could I really live my life daily so that I was constantly searching out the Lord's will and drawing on His grace to accomplish the task of becoming perfect? And when the Lord with His tender mercy meshes His power with my agency, and my effort and brings forth some measure of progress on the covenant path, I inquire, where is self-esteem? Where is even the need for self-esteem? Overwhelmed, I plead as the father who approached Christ with the desire that his son be healed: "Lord... Help thou mine unbelief" (Mark 9:24). Elder Enzio Busche warmly reassures us that we will recognize that we are growing in God-confidence and feeling the waves of such God-confidence crashing on the shores of our soul and replacing the undercurrents of self-confidence: This is the place where we suddenly see the heavens open as we feel the full impact of the love of our Heavenly Father, which fills us with indescribable joy. With this fulfillment of love in our hearts, we will never be happy anymore just by being ourselves or living our own lives. We will not be satisfied until we have surrendered our lives into the arms of the loving Christ, and until He has become the doer of all our deeds and He has become the speaker of all our words.[8]

When Jesus Christ is the doer of all our deeds and the speaker of all our words, I have to ask, "Where is 'self' "? Where is the need for self-confidence? I strongly suggest that self-confidence becomes a non-issue for the child of God who is perfecting his or her faith in the Lord Jesus Christ. We should desire to garner God-confidence by sacrificing misplaced self-confidence. The self can be so demanding that the only option seems to be that we jettison the pursuit of self-confidence in order to cleave unto the Lord (Omni 1:26). President Ezra Taft Benson invited us to be changed for Christ, captained by Christ, and consumed in Christ.[9] What is to be consumed we ask. I submit it to let go of our old concept of self-confidence, the one we learned from the precepts and philosophies of men. The pursuit of self-confidence might actually delay our having the might change of heart. Without our souls being filled with God-confidence, no amount of self-confidence or anything else can fill the void.

When considering how to approach that sacred process, it is helpful to view our desires from two perspectives: [1] Those desires that have already become righteous desires because they are aligned with God's desires; and [2] those desires that have not yet been aligned with God's desires. As to the first category, one might ask, "If our desires have been educated to be what Heavenly Father wants, then why do we need to continue educating them?" The answer seems to lie in the counsel King Benjamin gave to the members of the Church, "And now, for the sake of these things which I have spoken unto you—that is, for the sake of retaining a remission of your sins from day to day, that ye may walk guiltless before God" (Mosiah 4:26).

Once we have obtained and incorporated righteous desires in our hearts, it is necessary to continue to educate them through scripture study, prayer, and service in the kingdom with an eye single to the glory of God so that when the storms of adversity come, as they surely will, those desires will remain firmly and steadfastly anchored in the gospel's sod.[69] I'm reminded of something mentioned earlier in this book. After we pass through the veil into the spirit world, we will gaze on previously unseen vistas of the glory and grandeur of His work, leading to an expansion of our desires and further welding of our desires to His.

With regard to the second category, there are two subcategorizations: [1] unrighteous desires and [2] those desires associated with the cares of the world which appear to be righteous when viewed through the lens of mortality but are not aligned with God's will. Clearly, as we come to recognize "unrighteous" desires in our lives, they need to be eradicated and replaced with "righteous" desires. Two parables from the Savior are examples of these two subcategories of desires that are not aligned with God's desires. The first is the parable of the wedding feast and the man who prepared a supper, probably a Shabbat evening dinner.

> The kingdom of heaven is like unto a certain king, which made a marriage for his son, and sent forth his servants to call them that were bidden to the wedding [the king's desire]: and they would not come. Again, he sent forth other servants, saying, Tell them which are bidden, Behold, I have prepared my dinner: my oxen and my fatlings are killed, and all things are ready: come unto the marriage. But [now here are the unrighteous desires] they made light of it, and went their ways; one to his farm, another to his merchandise. (Matthew 22:2–5)

What is the source of making light and thinking that their desires are more important than the king's desire? Pride—the most treacherous of all unrighteous desires. Need more be said?

The second parable involves being invited to participate in a great feast.

> And sent his servant at supper time to say to them that were bidden, Come; for all things are now ready. And they all with one consent began to make excuse. The first said unto him, I have bought a piece of ground, and I must needs go and see it: I pray thee have me excused. And another said, I have bought five yoke of oxen, and I go to prove them: I pray thee have me excused. And another said, I have married a wife, and therefore I cannot come. (Luke 14:17–20)

In contrast to those invited to the wedding but declined with their flimsy and transparent excuses, those invited to the supper seem to have legitimate reasons for wanting to be excused. But they didn't realize that their desires, which on the surface seemed to be worthy and perhaps necessary, were not aligned with the Lord's desires.

Educating our unaligned desires involves jettisoning them so that the Lord can replace them with His desires. The Brother of Jared, having seen the finger of Jehovah, verbalized a bold desire, "Lord, show thyself unto me. And the Lord said unto him: "Believest thou the words that I *shall speak?*" (Ether 3:10–11, emphasis added). What an incredible learning criteria that was associated with the realization of that desire! The Brother of Jared was being asked to believe not only what the Lord *had already spoken to him,* but to believe in words that were *yet to be spoken,* not knowing what would be uttered. Educating our desires fits that pattern. Do we desire to see more, or are we content with what we have seen and really do not want the accountability associated with seeing more? Our Heavenly Father is asking that we exercise faith and believe in "what He shall speak" that will open our understanding and want to align our desire with His. In all likelihood, we probably not have fathomed the vastness of His interests and the specific, glorious desires with which He wants to align as we become more involved in His work of salvation of all His children. To have a genuine desire to submit to the desires and intents of God is best reflected in the words of a poem:

It is a difficult task when I kneel and pray and know I want things my very own way,
To wrench from my soul and falteringly say, "thy will be done."

But when I have said it and dried all my tears, I feel the assurance that silences fears.
I love him more deeply... more often can say—"Not my will, but thine, Lord. Yes, have thine own way.[11]

Notes

1. Neal A. Maxwell, "According to The Desires of [Our] Hearts," *Ensign*, November, 1996, 21.
2. Brigham Young, Journal of Discourses, 26 vols. (Liverpool: F. D. Richards, 1855), 2:123 (April 17, 1853).
3. Carol Lynn Pearson, *The Growing Season* (Salt Lake City: Bookcraft, Inc. 1976), 12–13, emphasis added.
4. Eugene England, "The Trouble with Excellence, or How to Value the 'Less Honorable' Gifts" (Salt Lake City: Deseret Book, 1984), 63–64.
5. Neal A Maxwell, "The Disciple-Scholar, Learning in the Light of Faith," a publication of lectures given to students in the Brigham Young University Honors Program (Salt Lake City: Bookcraft, Inc., 1995), 17–18.
6. As quoted by then Elder Henry B. Eyring of the Quorum of the Twelve in "The Disciple-Scholar, Learning in the Light of Faith," a publication of lectures given to students in the Brigham Young University Honors Program; Salt Lake City: Bookcraft, Inc. 1995, 53.
7. Ezra Taft Benson, "Cleansing the Inner Vessel," *Ensign*, May 1986, 6.
8. "Truth is the Issue," *Ensign*, Nov. 1993, 25.
9. See "Born of God," *Ensign*, July 1989, 5.
10. "I Believe in Christ," *Hymns*, no. 134.
11. Poem by Helen Campbell Monson, in the possession of the author.

CHAPTER 7
Desires to Strengthen Our Families

"Anchor your life in Jesus Christ, your Redeemer. Make your Eternal Father And His Beloved Son the most important priority in your life... Make their will your central desire."

—Richard G. Scott[1]

If a survey were conducted among members of the Church that contained the following question—"What would be your paramount desire for your family?" I am sure that the number one response, hands-down, would the same thing Lehi described during his vision of the tree of life.

> And as I cast my eyes round about, that perhaps I might discover my family... I beckoned unto them; and I also did say unto them with a loud voice that they should come unto me, and partake of the fruit, which was desirable above all other fruit. (1 Nephi 8:13–18)

Thus, in virtually every Church member's heart resides the desire for family members to be partakers of the incomparable fruit of the tree of life. Sadly, however, some are discouraged and distraught that, like Lehi's unquestionable righteous desire to have Laman and Lemuel come and partake, such a desire is unattainable. As a bishop, I lost count of the number of parents who lamented the unfulfilled desire to have their family members continually embracing the gospel and making progress toward becoming an eternal family. They lived in fear that they had failed in their responsibilities to "train up a child" and therefore were unworthy of Heavenly Father's blessings. There is great consolation in the words of Elder Robert D. Hales of the Quorum of the Twelve who spoke these assuring words:

> We should not let [our children's wayward] choices weaken our faith. Our worthiness will not be measured according to their [our children's] righteousness. Lehi [and Sariah] did not lose the blessing of feasting at the tree of life because Laman and Lemuel refused to partake of the fruit. Sometimes as parents we feel we have failed when our children make mistakes or stray. Parents are never failures when they do their best to love, teach, pray, and care for their children.[2]

It may take years and possibly even beyond the period of our mortal sojourn before the desire of seeing our children "walking in the light" is brought to fruition. But the oft-overlooked blessing of that unfulfilled desire is that we can feast on the fruit desirable above all others while we wait on the Lord, His purposes, and His timing.

After recounting his vision, Lehi expresses his fear that Laman and Lemuel "should be cast off from the presence of the Lord" (1 Nephi 8:36). Lehi's interpretation of his dream is framed by two central constructs: (1) being "cast off" and (2) being in "the presence of the Lord." Partaking of the sweetness, purity, and joy of coming unto the presence of the Lord does not require waiting until the end of our life. It is tremendously comforting and motivating to read the words of the prophet Helaman written to Captain Moroni, "And now, my beloved brother, Moroni, may the Lord our God, who has redeemed us and made us free, keep you continually in his presence" (Alma 58:41; emphasis added). As parents, we strive to teach our families the joy of living in our Heavenly Father's presence, and no matter their choices, do our best to stay in His presence while here on earth.

What, then, is to be understood regarding being "cast off?" Being "cast off" refers not only to the next life, but also to mortality. Individuals can cast themselves off spiritually, but tragically can choose to cast themselves off from mortality. Without question, each of us certainly desires to have the great blessings that come as a result of Jesus's atoning sacrifice, including comfort and peace when someone we know and love has cast themselves off into the next life. Our desire should be not to stress so much about the status of those who intentionally transferred themselves to the spirit world. We are better served, and it behooves us to remember, that God is in control and extends to us infinite mercy and compassion. So what about those who have passed on intentionally by taking their own lives?

Over the course of time, my life has been "rocked" by receiving the devastating news that someone close to me (six individuals) has committed suicide. I struggled with and wondered as to the status of these individuals with regard to "being in the presence of the Lord" or being "cast out." Over the years, I pondered from time to time about these circumstances and ultimately I developed a fervent desire to know the eternal standing for persons who take their lives. But, as is often said, when circumstances become personal, things change. In the spring 2012, I received word that my brother had committed suicide. He was raised in the Church just like me, been on a mission, and married in the temple. In his mid-forties, he became disenchanted with the Church and, for various reasons, was excommunicated. Then, in his early sixties, he had taken his life. My long-felt desire to know the status of those who take their lives as either being cast off or in the presence of the Lord suddenly became intense as I grieved his loss—not just for my sake and peace of mind, but for my two nieces (my brother's daughters) who were emotionally devastated by their father's precipitous action.

A few days after General conference in April 2014, I received a copy of a letter sent to my nieces from the temple department indicating that the First Presidency had authorized the President of the Salt Lake City temple to have my brother re-baptized and his temple blessings restored. Ten days later, I received a copy of the letter from the temple department confirming that the sacred, salvific ordinances had been re-performed vicariously in the Salt Lake Temple. My nieces were overjoyed beyond that which words can express. The pain, misery, and suffering were replaced by an encompassing peace.

I spent a considerable amount of time pondering this "miraculous" circumstance. Over the course of time wherein there was much pondering, the spirit confirmed five significant conclusions: (1) All barriers to my brother's eternal progression have been removed through the tender mercies of the atoning, infinite sacrifice of the Savior. (2) Even though saving ordinances are performed by the thousands in temples that dot the globe, we know that the person for whom these ordinances were performed must accept them by covenant in order for them to be efficacious. What kind of a process that those in the spirit world go through to accomplish this is still not known. (3) There is much forgiveness in the world of spirits. (4) My brother's status of either being in the presence of the Lord or being cut off from the presence of the Lord is not determined by his suicidal action. (5) His committing suicide is not a defining characteristic of his eternal possibilities.

I am convinced that there is a process inseparably connected to agency whereby persons accept the invitation and then covenant to abide by the vicarious ordinances performed through the operation of the priesthood on the earth, while they are in the spirit world. Whether my brother has re-accepted these ordinances and re-committed to his covenants again, I do not know. However, my desire to know the standing of those who take their life has been graciously and tenderly fulfilled. What comfort has been distilled upon my soul! My desire is like unto Lehi's—that my brother will choose to come and partake (again) of the fruit of the tree.

Now for the rest of the story... it turns out that the secretary to the Director of the Temple Department is my cousin. When I saw her for the first time in over forty years at a family reunion in August 2014, she shared with me the circumstances that triggered her sending the letters from the temple department. A few days after the April General Conference, President Monson met with the Director of the Temple Department indicating that he wanted the names of individuals who had been excommunicated from the Church and had also committed suicide in recent years. My brother's name was on that list. One of my deepest desires was to know that those who commit suicide are not "cast off" from the presence of the Lord, and that they can choose to resume keeping the commandments and continue on the path of eternal progression. God does not desire our separation from His presence. Our ultimate separation will be an expression of our own desires, not God's desires.

On the other end of the spectrum of family are those who have not yet been born. We have these comforting and deepening words from Joseph Smith who said in speaking of Bishop Newell K. Whitney, "Angels shall guard his house, and shall guard the lives of his posterity those yet unborn, and they shall become very great and very numerous on the earth."[3] Richard G. Ellsworth shared one of his spiritual experiences coming from one of his grandsons:

One day I helped one of my little grandsons in the bathroom with his needs. Perhaps feeling a bit embarrassed at my invasion of his three-and-a-half year old privacy, I hugged him up to me and said, "You know it is good for me to help you because I am big and you are little." He looked up at me with his big brown eyes and said in response, "I helped you when you were little." I remembered my training in childhood education and I replied in confidence, "Yes, I know. You were big when I was little and I am big when you are little." But he shook his head and looked up at me again; there was seriousness and wisdom in his eyes. He paused a moment and then said sweetly and clearly, "No, Grandpa. I mean before I was born, when you were little, I helped you." And then he added, "I liked helping you."[4]

Our desires were educated while in the premortal world. Those lessons so influenced our premortal self with the consequence that our self-perception here on earth reflects that education.

A final thought on the connection we have with those of our family who have paved the way before us is expressed by Elder John A. Widtsoe, "Whoever seeks to help those on the other side [meaning doing family history research and then going to the temple and getting the ordinances done] receives help in return in all the affairs of life."[5]

The vision of the tree of life clarifies the reality that agency is the final factor in our eternal status. The Book of Mormon emphasizes throughout its pages the godly desire for *all* (whether on this side of the veil or in the spirit world) to enjoy the presence of the Lord. "Come unto me and ye shall partake of the fruit of the tree of life" [Alma 5:34, see also verse 62]. The availability of the tree of life, as depicted in Lehi's dream, suggests that being in God's presence throughout eternity is offered to all of His children. This has to be the most tender of all mercies!

Another question many people have is, "What will our conversation with Jesus who is the 'keeper of the gate' (2 Nephi 9:41) entail?" In June 1965, a group of brethren in the Physical Facilities Department were doing repair work outside the Hotel Utah apartment of President and Sister McKay. One morning, as President McKay stepped through the door, he stopped to thank them for their labors. Then he paused and taught them the importance of family relationships and especially those relationships with each child in the family:

Let me assure you, Brethren, that each of you will have a personal priesthood interview with the Savior Himself. If you are interested,

I will tell you the order in which He will ask you to account for your earthly responsibilities... He will want an accountability report about each of your children individually. He will not attempt to have this for simply a family stewardship report but will request information about your relationship to each and every child.[6]

The priority that should be allocated to each child is poignantly illustrated in the following lines shared by Vaughn J. Featherstone,

When Mike was two he wanted a sandbox and his father said, "There goes the yard. We will have kids over here day and night, and they will throw sand into the flower beds, and cats will make a mess on it, and it'll kill the grass for sure."

Mike's mother said, "It'll come back."

When Mike was five, he wanted a jungle gym with swings that would take his breath away and bars to take him to the summit. His father said, "Good grief, I've seen those things in back yards, and do you know what those lawns look like? Mud holes in a pasture. Kids digging their shoes in the ground! It'll kill the grass."

Mike's mother said, "It will come back."

Between breaths when daddy was blowing up the plastic swimming pool he warned, "You know what they are going to do to this place? They are going to condemn it and use if for a missile site. They'll track water everywhere and have a million water fights, and you won't be able to take out the garbage without stepping into mud up to your neck. When we take this down, we will have the only brown lawn on the block."

Mike's mother said, "It will come back."

When Mike was twelve, he volunteered his yard for the scout camp out. As they hoisted their tents and drove in the spikes, his father stood and the window and observed, "Why don't I just put the grass seed out in cereal bowls for the birds and save myself the trouble of spreading it around? You know for a fact that those tents and all those big feet are going to trample down every single blade of grass, don't you.

Don't bother to answer; I know what you are going to say—"It will come back."

The basketball hoop on the side of the garage attracted more crowds than the Olympics. And a small patch of lawn that started out with a barren spot the size of a garbage can lid soon grew to encompass the entire side yard. Just when it looked as if the new seed might take root, winter came and the sled runners beat it into ridges. Mike's father shook his head and said, "I never asked for much in this life—only a patch of grass."

And his wife smiled and said. "It will come back."

The lawn this fall is beautiful. It was green and alive and rolled out like a sponge carpet along the drive where gym shoes had trod... along the garage where bicycles used to fall... and around the flower beds where little boys used to dig with their iced-tea spoons. But Mike's father never saw it. He anxiously looked beyond the yard and asked with a catch in his voice,

"Mike will come back, won't he?"[7]

As parents do we desire "patches of grass" in our lives rather than providing each child with the spiritual and eternity-centered experiences that will cause them to come back, both to us and our Heavenly Father? One of the particularly haunting questions in all of scripture is found in Genesis 44:34. Reuben was the oldest of the twelve sons of Jacob (Israel) and had sold Joseph into slavery. This same Joseph was now second in command to the Pharaoh in all of Egypt and had decreed that Benjamin must stay while the other ten brothers return to Israel to bring the rest of the family to Egypt to survive the famine. Reuben's reply has a far deeper meaning than he realized at the time: "How can I go up to my father and the lad not be with me?" Do we really desire to do everything in our power as parents, short of infringing on agency, to ensure that we can go up to our Father in Heaven and have our children with us? I sometimes wonder this question as I wander through a park and see mothers or fathers buried in social media on their smartphones, totally oblivious to their children on the playground. Somehow, in a weird rationalization, those parents think that taking their children to the part counts, when playing with them is what really matters. My heart is pained as I see people being sucked into the terrible trap of selfishness that social media creates.

Desire to "Plow in Hope"

In his epistle to strengthen the Corinthian Saints, Paul writes, "he that ploweth should plow in hope" (1 Corinthians 9:10). For many parents and children, the cultivation and sustaining of hope in today's world seems overwhelming and possibly fruitless. There is no doubt that the world is in "commotion" (See Doctrine and Covenants 45:26) as prophesied by the Lord himself. But the good news is that the kingdom of God on earth is in forward motion (the Lord is hastening his work) as never before because the valiant among us keep moving forward in spite of the maelstroms surrounding us, including the pernicious attacks on the traditional constructs, values, and definitions associated with marriage and family. True, we have unprecedented mass entertainment and mass communication, but so many lonely crowds. The togetherness of technology is an unsatisfactory substitute for the family. Those who plow in hope not only understand the law of the harvest, but they also recognized what growing seasons are all about, and with the "eye of faith" (Alma 5:15) continually bring into sharper focus the divine design for families and eternal companionships. Those who plow in hope also choose to yield to the highest Sovereign. They have discovered that putting off the natural man makes possible putting on the whole armor of God, which would not fully fit prior to jettisoning the ways of the world and rejecting the wiles of Satan (see Ephesians 6:11, 13) The Book of Ether describes conditions under King Lib, who among other things, caused his people to "make all manner of tools to till the earth, both to plow and sow, to reap and hoe, and also to thrash" (Ether 10:25). Although this Book of Mormon text is describing tools of physical survival, namely planting, cultivating, and harvesting crops for food, symbolically we see that there are important tools (a.k.a armor) that parents and children need to survive spiritually and to live "after the manner of happiness" (2 Nephi 5:27).

Notes

1. Richard G. Scott, "The Power of Correct Principles", *Ensign*, May 1988, 4.
2. Robert D Hales, "With All the Feeling of a Tender Parent: A Message of Hope to Families," *Conference Report*, April 2004, 90.
3. Newell K. Whitney, "The Personal Writings of Joseph Smith" ed. Dean C. Jessee (Salt Lake City: Deseret Book, 1984), 62.
4. Richard G. Ellsworth, "Spiritual Experience," BYU Speeches 1985, 23 July 1985.
5. John A Widtsoe, "Genealogical Activities in Europe", Utah Genealogical and Historical Magazine, 22 July 1931, 104; emphasis added.
6. From the notes of Fred A. Baker, Managing Director, Department of Physical Facilities as quoted by Robert D. Hales, BYU Speeches, March 15, 1988.
7. Erma Bombeck, as quoted by Vaughn J. Featherstone in "The Impact Teacher," *Ensign*, Nov. 1976.

CHAPTER 8
Desire to Become Un-fallen

"To him [or her] that overcometh [become unfallen] will I make a pillar in the temple of my God."

—Revelation 3:12

I have been blessed with opportunities to travel in more than fifty countries around the world. In such places as the United Kingdom, Italy, Greece, China, Tibet, and Egypt, I have seen many magnificent man-made temples, some of which are still standing as tributes to the incredible skill and artistry of architects and engineers. Most impressive to me are the pillars that formed the infra-super structure of these remarkable monuments. I stood in awe of the beauty of these pillars anchored firmly to solid foundations, still standing as testaments to the builders supporting the porticoes, ceilings, roofs, and walls of the temple. Sadly, many other pillars had toppled over and broken into pieces lying on the ground either by the destructive forces of nature or by the hand of pillaging vandals. The symbolism of God making the righteous "temple pillars" has flowed into my mind on these occasions. The temple teaches us the true purpose of the Fall and why we desired to come to a fallen world. There we are taught the plan of salvation, including the key stepping stones designed to fulfill our desire to become un-fallen and be able to re-enter our heavenly home.

When people join the Church, they are enrolling in the Lord's university where the curriculum of eternal life is taught. We make additional covenants beyond those we brought with us from our heavenly home. We are placed again on the covenant path that will lead us to rejoin and live with our Heavenly Parents and our eternal family. However, like most universities, there is a graduate school. The temple and its pillars are the Lord's graduate school. In the process of participating in the ordinances therein, which are a continuation along the covenant path—the path that began in the premortal life—we are taught the sacred purposes of the Creation and the Fall. As important as those understandings are, of equal worth is knowledge gained about how to become "un-fallen." In sum, the temple is the campus for educating our desires.

Arguably, temples and temple worship are among the unique aspects of The Church of Jesus Christ of Latter-day Saints. Soon, more than 160 operating temples will dot the earth. Surely, the stone cut of a mountain without hands and breaking into smaller stones is covering the earth.

One of our Mormon jargon sayings concerning temple activity no doubt confuses and mystifies those not of our faith—namely, "I am going through the temple" or "I went through the temple." Multi-varied visions of what these phrases mean are construed in the minds of non-believers and certainly leave room for much misunderstanding. As important as it is for each of us to "go through the temple and receive our own washing, anointing, and endowment," returning frequently to perform those salvific ordinances for those who have left mortality and now reside in the world of spirits, there is a much more significant element of this "sacrament" which can be succinctly stated by the question: "Did the temple go through me?" Would it not be more appropriate and descriptive to refer to the unique activity of worshipping Father in Heaven by saying, "I worshipped at the temple and received those ordinances which qualify me to receive an endowment of divine power from my Father in Heaven as I honor the covenants and commitments I made as part of the temple ceremonies"? Now, I know that I will never be able to rid the phrase "gone through the temple and received my endowments" from Latter-day Saint culture. But perhaps we can more frequently re-translate that expression so as to convey more clarity and diffuse mystery and misunderstanding. Such would be a most noble desire, since the purpose of the temple is to help us become un-fallen.

As a reference point for the discussion contained in this chapter, I refer to the words of Jehovah himself on the occasion of instructing

Joseph and the Saints in Ohio regarding the necessity (and I should point out, the means) of building the Kirtland Temple. "Yea, verily I say unto you, I gave unto you a commandment that you should build a house, in the which house *I design to endow you with power from on high; for this is the promise of the Father unto you*" (Doctrine and Covenants 95:8–9, emphasis added). How significant! How magnificent! The Father promised Jehovah that He would endow power upon His disciples in the fledgling restored Church if they prepared a physically sacred place; and, as later described, presented a spiritually ready Saint who would be worthy to enter the temple and partake of the incomprehensible blessings therein. Truman Madsen wrote,

> We are to receive IN temples, THROUGH temples and FROM temples, POWER FROM ON HIGH. Christ is the source of that power. The temples are his; and every symbol in and out of those sacred structures points toward him; and, as a cup carries water, transmit the Spirit of Jesus Christ.[1]

Consider for a moment those occasions when you have been invited to someone's home for the first time. Almost subconsciously, we observe every minute detail about our friend's home because, in large measure, the way it is decorated, painted, landscaped, cared for, and so on, is a reflection of the kind of person our friends are and tells us something about their value system. We learn much about people by in and around and going through their homes. (Now, good sisters, don't get paranoid that every time the bishop or priesthood / Relief Society ministers come by to visit that they are thinking, "I wonder what we will learn about Brother and Sister So-and-So tonight.")

But is it not reasonable that the Lord's temples, which are constructed "not after the manner of the world" (Doctrine and Covenants 95:13) can reveal to us many things concerning the nature, power, purposes, plans, and ways of our Father in Heaven. In fact, I submit that Heavenly Father intends that we not merely learn OF or ABOUT Christ in the temple. Rather, we will to come to KNOW him and move forward in BECOMING like him. We will be instructed more fully to know that his "only interest" is to bring about the immortality and eternal life of man. Temples provide such cosmic glimpses.

We gain an insight that would have been lost forever had Joseph not corrected the wording of the New Testament passage regarding Judgment Day, wherein many will say, "Lord, Lord, did we not do this and that (i.e. good works) in thy name?" Jesus' reply according to the King James Version of the text says, "I never knew you" (Matthew 7:23). However, Joseph's Inspired Version renders the Messiah's response as "You never knew me" (JST, Matthew 7:23). I would postulate that we cannot KNOW Christ unless we regularly attend the temple and come to recognize his attributes, character, desires, and passions. An expanded knowledge of Christ will be the natural consequence of our spending time in His house and gaining the further light and knowledge that emanates from within those sacred walls. Jehovah himself told Enoch, "And behold...all things are created and made to bear record of me, both things which are temporal and things which are spiritual; things which are in the heavens above, and things which are on the earth, and things which are in the earth; and things which are under the earth; both above and beneath: all things bear record of me" (Moses 6:63, emphasis added].

What I desire to do is examine some perspectives that will enhance our understanding of temples (i.e., the temple will go through me) and thus contribute to our knowing Christ better and pushing us along the straight and narrow path that leads to becoming like Him. Imagine how uncomfortable you felt the first time you visited the home of someone you did not know. Similar phenomenon and feelings will occur on Judgment Day, when we are asked to report and indicate to Jesus (the gatekeeper) which kingdom we are prepared to enter. It will be impossible to enter a celestial home if we do not know and become like the creator of that home—the one who came to earth, performed the Atonement, and then rose to heaven that He might prepare a residence for us among His many mansions. Recall the Savior's words, "I go to prepare a place for you" (John 14:2). Most would infer that the "place" being prepared is our heavenly residence where we will live after completing our mission here. But I think that the Savior has prepared a "place" for us while we endure the vicissitudes of mortality. That place, of course, is the temple. My desire is that we will no longer view temple attendance as "temple work," or that we have gone through or are going through the temple. Rather, I sincerely hope that the temple will go through us and that continued attendance will become temple worship generating within each of a never ending desire to know and become like Jehovah, our Redeemer.

As the foundation for overcoming and breaking down barriers that inhibit or impede the temple from going through us, I relate an incident from the life of President David O. McKay. On the occasion of his announcing the construction of the Los Angeles Temple, he told a large gathering of Saints about his niece who, short after being inducted into a sorority on the campus of a large university she was attending, had participated in temple ordinances for the first time. President McKay's niece asked her uncle for an interview shortly after both of these incidents had taken place. At the appointed time, the niece confessed that the temple ceremony was a disappointment compared to the elaborate ritual associated with being inducted into the sorority. President McKay stunned the congregation with his response to his niece.

> I was disappointed in the temple. And then he hastened to add, gesturing to the vast congregation gathered for the announcement, And you were too! WHY were we disappointed? Because we were unprepared! We had stereotypes in our minds and faulty expectations. We were unable to distinguish the symbol from the symbolized. We were not worthy enough. We were inclined to respond negatively and critically. We were not seasoned spiritually." Continuing, he shed this insight, "I believe that there are few persons—(remember that President McKay was 80 years old at that time and had been in the temple every Thursday for over fifty years) even temple workers, who really comprehend the full meaning and power of the endowment."[2]

Given that premise, let's analyze the barriers identified by President McKay that preclude the temple from going through us and see how we might overcome them so that we might see the fulfillment of our desire to become "a pillar in the temple" (Revelation 3:12).

Desire to be Better Prepared When We Go to the Temple

First, I suggest that we study the scriptures, carefully selecting and concentrating on those pertaining to the temple. Almost three hundred references exist to temples in the Doctrine and Covenants alone. Obviously, time and space will not permit us to examine those. Instead, perhaps a couple from the Book of Psalms in the Old Testament will be helpful. Written by David, who had at one point, had an incredible love for temples, especially since he petitioned Jehovah on multiple occasions and finally received permission and approval from the Lord to build a temple in Jerusalem. He was given inspiration to select the site for the first permanent worship structure, contracted with various merchants, primarily Phoenicians for materials and laborers to construct the temple. However, David did not remain worthy to the covenants associated with this divine assignment; and so it was left to his son Solomon to complete and dedicate the massive undertaking. Many scholars believe that Psalms or "Songs of Praise," as they are called in Hebrew is a manual of temple worship. For instance, the twenty-fourth Psalm could constitute a temple recommend interview for someone desiring to enter the temple. "Who shall ascend into the hill of the Lord?" (Psalm 24:3). Other examples include, "But as for me, I will come into thy house in the multitude of thy mercy: and in thy fear [love] will I worship toward thy holy temple. Lead me, O Lord, in thy righteousness." (Psalms 5:7–8, emphasis added) Finally, "I will worship toward thy holy temple, and praise thy name for they lovingkindness and for thy truth" (Psalms 138:2, emphasis added).

Second, we can be less hasty as we go to the temple. What can we do to be in less of a rush to arrive at the temple, fumbling to be sure our recommends are current and in our possession, or that we have our temple clothing? There is no indication that Christ rushed through the process of creating the world. There is no sense of uncontrolled urgency as He orchestrates the instructional and melodic curriculum prepared for Adam, Eve, and their posterity. Why should we be in a hurry?

Third, what could we learn about Christ if we spent ten to fifteen minutes standing or walking slowly around the grounds and looking at the exterior of the Lord's house? Surely there is more that we can come to know about Jehovah by gazing upon the handiwork of those who constructed man-made "mountains of the Lord" both in the architecture of the temple buildings and in the graceful and delicate hand of Mother Nature reflected in the heavenly landscaping. Isn't it possible that women had input during the creation of this earth with its ten thousand flowers? Consider the beauty of the creation process as portrayed in the temple presentation. Mother Nature is certainly a more appropriate moniker than Father Nature. That women were involved in the creative and organization processes associated with the formation of our mortal home is alluded to in the revelation given to President Joseph F. Smith, who was pondering the activities in the spirit world.

> Thus it was made known that our Redeemer spent his time during his sojourn in the world of spirits, instructing and preparing the faithful spirits of the prophets who had testified of him in the flesh; that they might carry the message of redemption unto all the dead, unto whom He could not go personally, because of their rebellion and transgression, that they through the ministration of his servants might also hear his

words. Among the great and mighty ones who were assembled in this vast congregation of the righteous were Father Adam, the Ancient of Days and father of all, our glorious Mother Eve, with many of her faithful daughters who have lived through the ages and worshipped the true and living God." (Doctrine and Covenants 138:36–39, emphasis added)

Just as righteous sisters are involved in the great and marvelous missionary process among the dead, I believe that they were also valiant participants when the "gods" organized the world.

We should also remember that the Garden of Eden was the first temple. Elohim and Jehovah regularly visited the Garden, but that after the transgression of partaking of the forbidden fruit, Adam and Eve had to leave the presence of the Lord and begin the process of preparation, instruction, and covenant-making in order to return and dwell again in His presence. Shouldn't we pause to ponder and absorb the simple beauty of the celestial room after completing an endowment session?

Forgive a personal note here, but I have always taken occasion whenever possible when I have had the opportunity to go to any temple to ask to be able to step into the baptistery, particularly when the font rests on the backs of twelve oxen, representing the Twelve Tribes of Israel. Why? Because my father once had the assignment to paint the twelve oxen in the Salt Lake Temple baptistery with gold leaf. It has always been a source of strength to me to visualize his painstaking efforts to paint an acceptable offering of beauty in holiness as David had prayed when making offerings unto the Lord: "Give unto the Lord the glory due unto his name: bring an offering and come before him: worship the Lord in the beauty of his holiness" (1 Chronicles 16:29).

Desire to Increase Our Spirituality and Humility

We are afflicted and tormented by our imperfections which generate in our minds a mistaken notion of perhaps being unworthy in varying degrees to attend the temple and be endowed with power from on high. In some cases, we are not all that anxious to change (repent). We are like St. Augustine who uttered the prayer: " Lord, make me pure, but not yet."[3] The gospel requires that the saints sacrifice all earthly things in order to achieve what Joseph Smith called "faith unto exaltation."[4] The Lord asks us to sacrifice our sins and transgressions upon the altar now, but we frequently discover that our favorite imperfections are the most difficult to sacrifice. The temple recommend process is our opportunity to "return and report" our progress (or perhaps the lack thereof) to the Lord through his authorized agents, in adding to our character the finest qualities exemplified during the perfect mortal life of our Elder Brother. We "bring them word," as it were, of our accomplishments and progress made in eternally significant assignments. We receive instructions and encouragement resulting in renewed dedication and commitment to honor our covenants so that we can receive an endowment of further light and knowledge promised as a consequence of keeping those sacred covenants so that we can receive an endowment of further light and knowledge necessary to drive Satan and his evil influences from of our lives. For those who are sometimes overwhelmed with feelings that imperfections cast doubt on your worthiness to attend the temple, consider the following marvelous uplifting statement from Brigham Young.

> Those who do right and seek the glory of Father in Heaven, whether their knowledge be little or much, or whether they can do little or much, if they do the very best they know how, they are perfect...be as perfect as you can, for that is all we can do [even] tho' it is written, "Be ye therefore perfect as your Father who is in Heaven and I are perfect." To be as perfect as we possibly can, according to our knowledge, is to be just as perfect as Father in Heaven is. He cannot be any more perfect than he knows how to, any more than we can. When we are doing as well as we know how in the sphere and station which we occupy here, we are justified.[5]

Desire to Discern the Symbolism of Ritual and Ceremony

Each of the gospel's saving ordinances (especially those performed in the temples) are channels of divine power and heavenly knowledge. The Lord revealed in our dispensation, "the power of godliness are manifest" in the ordinances (Doctrine and Covenants 84:20). This statement is particularly true when referring to temple ordinances. Sometimes, the presence and performance of ritual and ceremony can be distracting, particularly if we do not maintain proper perspective. Consider the following circumstance recounted by Elder Boyd K. Packer:

> A number of years ago, I served on a stake high council in Brigham City (Utah, USA). On one occasion, the stake presidency and members of the high council and their wives attended an evening session in the Logan Temple. One of the temple workers was participating in the

endowment session as a worker for the first time and did very poorly. He had difficulty remembering his part (this was in the years before the video when temple workers "acted" out the scenes now displayed in the video) and was obviously nervous and flustered. He mixed up the presentation in a way that in other [settings] would have been considered humorous. He struggled through, however, and was gently coached and corrected by those who were serving with him on the session. As much dignity and reverence was maintained as would be possible considering his difficulty. After the session was over, the Brethren from the stake presidency and high council were standing on the walkway waiting for their wives to join them. One of the brethren commented in some amusement that he surely would not have wanted to be that man that night. "He really went through an ordeal. It was like being put on trial before all those patrons." The stake president, characteristically a quiet man, said with some firmness, "Hold on, brethren, let's get one thing straight here. It wasn't that man that was on trial here tonight. We were."[6]

My own service as a temple ordinance worker reinforced that lesson. I discovered how challenging it is to stay focused and perform the actions and ordinances and say the words perfectly—which is the goal in performing the endowment—session after session. Obviously, the first few times we watch the video presentation, it holds our attention. But the tendency, especially after hundreds of repeated viewings (which is the situation that temple ordinance workers encounter) is not to concentrate and to fall in to what I would call "mobile-device stupor." Similarly, the actions associated with the giving and receiving of tokens and signs of the Holy priesthood, and the other ordinances that are an integral part of the process established to become saviors on Mount Zion for our kindred dead can become routine and perfunctory and lose their meaning if we do not look for the deeper spiritual messages which they represent.

We are well served by something that Elder Orson F. Whitney said and that had been posted as a placard on one of the walls in the Salt Lake Temple: "God teaches by symbols; it is his favorite method of teaching."[7] To be fluent in the language of the Spirit, one must be fluent in the language of symbolism. One technique that I have found helpful in this challenging by meaningful mental exercise is to try to associate each of the symbols with Christ, His attributes, or His actions in some manner. Professor Joseph Fielding McConkie (BYU) set the tone for this approach: "Symbols are the timeless and universal language by which God, in His wisdom, has chosen to... bear witness of his [only begotten] Son."[8] Elder John A. Widtsoe addressed the importance of understanding symbols,

> We live in a world of symbols. We know nothing except by symbols. We make a few marks on a sheet of paper and say that they form a word which stands for LOVE, HATE, CHARITY, or ETERNITY. The marks may not be very beautiful to the eye. No one finds fault with the symbols on the pages of a book [or computer screen] just because they are not as mighty in their own beauty as the things which they represent. We do not quarrel with the symbol G-O-D because it is not very beautiful, yet it represents the majesty of God. We are glad to have symbols, if only the meaning of the symbols is brought home to us...No man or woman can come out of the temple endowed as he/she should be, unless he/she has seen beyond the symbol, the mighty realities for which the symbols stand.[9]

In another sense, a loving and wise Heavenly Father imbeds the true meanings and messages of the endowment in symbolism not only to preserve the sacred, but also to protect us, as it were, from receiving light and knowledge for which we become immediately accountable, until we are prepared to accept it and to abide covenants to follow it. Even though the meaning of temple symbols may not distill on us immediately, we can see and appreciate their beauty knowing that they were created to transmit eternal principles of how Father in Heaven works with in an unceasing process of saving His children. Our kindred dead deserve our perfect performance and our undivided attention to the proceedings of the temple endowment and related ordinances. They have waited a long time. Besides, remember is it that person's (for whom we are acting as proxy) first time to witness and partake of the ordinances. President Wilford Woodruff who dedicated the Salt Lake Temple taught that "there will be few if any who will not receive the ordinances of the temple when they are performed for them."[10] It is totally consistent with the Lord's stated purpose (see Moses 1:39) that virtually all the ordinances presently being performed in the temples are being accepted and become efficacious in the lives of those beyond the veil—even more reason to concentrate on the messages and meanings of temple ritual and ceremony. What assurance, peace, comfort, and love for those who have preceded us to the next phase of our existence, fills our heart to realize that in just two hours a convert has been placed again onto the covenant path of eternal progression.

Desire to See the Temple as the Link Between Heaven and Earth

Truman G. Madsen wrote, "The temple ceremonies represent the Lord's graduate course in learning to subdue the earth and mortal tendencies. It is the key to mastery over the temporal earth and our temporal nature."[11] The Master Teacher frequently used questions to evoke understanding in His disciples. One of his most soul-piercing one was, "Therefore, what manner of men [and women] ought ye to be? Verily, I say unto you, even as I am" (3 Nephi 27:27). Our Heavenly Father designed the symbolism of temple ritual and ceremony to teach us about His ways and His thoughts. Are we to remain in darkness not comprehending, as did ancient Israel in not recognizing that the underlying purpose of the various components of the Law of Moses was to be a schoolmaster to *bring* and *draw* them to Christ? Thus, we having been *brought* to Christ through baptism and receiving of the Holy Ghost are to view the temple as the *gate* to *heaven*, opening previously unseen vistas for us to *know* Christ. Elder John Widtsoe, a former member of the Quorum of the twelve taught:

> There are four stages to the temple endowment, which fully maximize the utilization of our agency—(1) the preparatory ordinances; (2) the visual presentations; (3) the covenants, and (4) the tests of knowledge. The instructions associated with the initiatory ordinances of washing and anointing prepare us for further light and knowledge regarding the Creation of the world, the creation and nature of man, the Fall, the Atonement, and the divine process of receiving Christ's infinite sacrifice in order to be redeemed from ALL the effects of the Fall. We accept such light and knowledge by binding ourselves with covenants. Then, through faithfulness to those covenants, we receive additional light and knowledge as we converse with the Lord at the veil and demonstrate our knowledge and understandings gained during the endowment process.[12]

Each of these stages is intended to educate our desires so that God can align them (because that is what we want to do) with the great plan of happiness. Exercising our agency, we become co-contributors to the process of making the Atonement of Jesus Christ the objective of our daily efforts. Steve Covey writes,

> It seems to me that the temple endowment experience is akin to Moses' experience. I see it at one of the Lord's great efforts to give man a correct

map of him / herself and of our purposes in mortality...The divine mirror of the temple endowment (provides) an accurate map of man's nature emerging from the [human] social mirror. These celestial principles and goals are as different from the best principles and goals which modern philosophy or psychology can suggest to man as the sun is from the moon. Any effort to use a secular frame of reference or (man-made) map to evaluate man's celestial/eternal map (as presented in the temple) would be comparable to holding a flashlight up to get a better view of the sun.[13]

Desire to Adjust Our Expectations

Joseph Smith once said, "The Saints expect to see some wonderful manifestation, some great display of power or some extraordinary miracle performed."[14] So it is with the temple; some of us go unrealistically expecting spectacular manifestations of God's powers and glory. Perhaps we even expect supernatural displays of celestial pyrotechnics. But what we find is simple ceremony, filled with repetition and ritual. Why? Joseph Smith continues, "Lest [we] become puffed up with pride and fall under condemnation, apply yourselves diligently to study that your minds be may be stored with all necessary information."[15] Although the Prophet's context is obtaining gospel knowledge from the meticulous study of revealed word—both former days and modern day—it applies equally well to gaining knowledge available in the temple.

Having the temple go through us stores additional power and knowledge in our minds and hearts, refining and refocusing desires. So we ask, what is the necessity of continual study? Why can't the Holy Ghost provide instant understanding? What is the purpose of attending the temple over and over? Can't the one-time influence of the Spirit be sufficient? Unfortunately, the response to each of these questions is a resounding NO. There is no cram course, no quickie set of Cliff Notes, nor an internet app to knowing Christ. Joseph concludes,

> We recognize that God has created men and women with minds capable of [instantaneously and fully retentive] instruction, and a faculty which may be enlarged in proportion to the heed and diligence given to the light communicated from the heavens to the intellect... but... NO MAN / WOMAN EVER ARRIVED IN A MOMENT. WE MUST BE INSTRUCTED IN PROPER DEGREES.[16]

Joseph is lovingly teaching each of us, in essence, that no short cut exists to learning the gospel and gaining knowledge of God and His ways, especially as it pertains to the sacred messages of the temple endowment. Likewise, there is no crash course available when pursuing the Lord's graduate curriculum contained in temple ordinances. Learning takes place grace for grace (Doctrine and Covenants 93:12–13), by degrees and in properly priority. The Lord does not shower or pour out one dose of his knowledge hoping somehow we will retain and understand the optimal/maximal amount necessary to result in our redemption and exaltation. Rather, He established ordinances, particularly those performed in temples, to allow us learn by degree until we come to the fullness. Like Christ, we will find ourselves growing from grace to grace, learning line upon line (2 Nephi 28:30). Every time I attend the temple desiring to obtain additional knowledge and understanding, I hear, see, or notice something not previously observed. Such is the divine process of educating our desires.

Conclusion

President Harold B. Lee once said, "In the temple, we are close to the Lord. Where is He more likely to be than here in His house?" On more than one occasion during the years of my assignment as an ordinance worker, as I sat in one of the instruction rooms, or walked down a hallway headed to where I would perform my next assignment, the thought entered my mind that Jesus Christ has actually physically walked through this sacred space. I was overwhelmed with awe and wonder that God would allow us mortals to enter, serve, and to be spiritually seasoned in his holy house. Ponder the words of Elder John A. Widtsoe spoken in General Conference,

> Men [and women] may rise through temple work to high levels of [Christ-like] character and spiritual joy. Once only may a person receive the temple endowment for him [or her] self; but innumerable times we may receive it for those who have gone from the earth. Whenever [we] do, we perform an unselfish act for which no earthly recompense is available. We taste in part the sweet joy of savior-hood. We rise toward the stature of the Lord Jesus Christ who died for all.[17]

In what more meaningful manner could Jesus teach us what being a savior is like other than by inviting us to act as proxy for those who have gone before? Joseph Smith taught that when we enter the spirit world, those persons for whom we have acted as proxy and participated in temple ordinances will fall at our feet and shed tears of joy and will clasp our knees in hugs of loving joy for our providing them with the opportunity to accept the eternal covenants of the gospel, the blessings of the endowment, and the sealing of families together forever. Let us educate our desire to have the temple go through us and become pillars of the temple by

- Increasing our preparedness
- Improving our worthiness
- Discerning the messages of ritual and ceremony
- Recognizing the temple as the link between heaven and earth
- Eliminating stereotypes and faulty or unrealistic expectations
- Distinguishing between the symbol and the symbolized
- Becoming more spiritually seasoned

"Seen for what it is, the [endowment] is a step-by-step ascent into the Eternal Presence of God."[18]

Notes

1. Truman Madsen, *The Highest In Us* (Salt Lake City: Bookcraft, Inc. 1978).
2. Truman Madsen, *The Radiant Life* (Salt Lake City: Bookcraft, Inc. 1994).
3. St. Augustine, "Lord, Make Me Pure But Not Yet—Augustine's Wayward Prayer," Church History Review, October 15, 2008.
4. Lectures on Faith, Lecture Sixth
5. Brigham Young, "Discourse," Deseret News Weekly, 31, August, 1854.
6. *Teach Ye Diligently* (Salt Lake City: Desert Book Company, 1975), 275.
7. Orson F. Whitney, *Improvement Era*, August 1927, 861.
8. *Gospel Symbolism* (Salt Lake City, Bookcraft, Inc. 1995), 1.
9. John A. Widtsoe, "Temple Worship," address given at a meeting of the Genealogical Society of Utah, Assembly Hall in Salt Lake City, October 12, 1920.
10. Wilford Woodruff, *Discourses of Wilford Woodruff*, ed. G. Homer Durham (Salt Lake City, Deseret Book, 1946), 158.
11. *The Highest in Us* (Salt Lake City: Bookcraft, Inc. 1978), 97.
12. John A. Widtsoe, "Temple Worship," lecture given to the Utah

Genealogical Society of Utah in the Assembly Hall, Temple Square, Salt Lake City, Utah, October 12, 1920.

13. Steve Covey, *The Divine Center* (Salt Lake City: Bookcraft, Inc. 1982), 175–6.

14. *Teachings of the Prophet Joseph Smith*, comp. Joseph Fielding Smith (Salt Lake City, Deseret Book, 1976), 51.

15. Ibid.

16. Ibid.

17. John A. Widtsoe, *Improvement Era*, April 1936, 228.

18. David O. McKay, as quoted in Andrew Ehat's "Who Shall Ascend into the Hill of the Lord? Sesquicentennial Reflections on a Sacred Day" May 4, 1842 in "Temples of the Ancient World" Neal A. Maxwell Institute for Religious Scholarship, 1994.

CHAPTER 9
Desire to Conquer Problems

"Endure the crosses of the world... and waste [not] the days of your probation.

—2 Nephi 9:18, 27

It goes without saying that everyone has problems. Dealing with our uniquely tailored problems can often have unintended consequences. For instance, the overwhelming nature of and seemingly constant barrage of problems can frustrate us, thus reducing the intensity of our desires to endure, or like the "mists of darkness" in Lehi's dream, we either abandon our desires or we become distracted and lose our focus. The objective of this chapter is to recognize the interconnectedness of works and desires. We find ourselves in this mortal laboratory full of enthusiasm to have our desires educated only to find that the learning activities involve problems and challenges. Therefore, at first it seems a bit unusual and perhaps even not aligned or consistent with the gospel to desire the "crosses of the world." By substituting the word "mortality" for "world," we are led to a much more insightful conclusion. We desired to be born into mortality knowing that it would be full of challenges, some of our choosing, some by way of pre-earth life assignment, or just the vagaries and vicissitudes of a fallen world.

Several years ago, I had occasion to be at an Institute of Religion. Near the entrance to one of the lecture auditoriums, I could not help but notice a giant poster displayed on the wall. It had a black background with large red letters spelling out the word *problems* vertically down the left-hand side of the poster. To the right of each letter in the word *problems* was a single word characterizing a certain aspect of problems, along with a short sentence or two of explanation, all in white letters. Intrigued by what that poster communicated about eight dimensions of problems, I found a piece of paper and copied down the following:

PREDICTORS	Responses to our problems mold our future
REMINDERS	Problems are reminders that we are not self-sufficient. We need God and others to help us overcome them.
OPPORTUNITIES	Problems pull us out of ruts and provide opportunities to think creatively
BLESSINGS	Problems open doors we usually wouldn't go through if left to our own desires and choices
LESSONS	Each new problem becomes a teacher. What is in question is the kind of student we are going to be
EVERYWHERE	No place or person is excluded from having problems
MESSAGES	Problems are warnings about potential disaster
SOLVABLE	No problem is without a solution

Let us explore each of these elements by considering several examples and personal experiences with problems and crosses as tutors of our desires that all might be edified and endure in righteousness.

Our Responses Mold Our Future in Accordance with God's Desires

Like it or not, for better or worse, the composite of what we are today is a direct consequence of how we have either conquered our problems (a.k.a endured the crosses of mortality) or they have conquered us. Lehi outlines the framework of operation when dealing with problems / crosses when he said, "We are free forever, knowing good from evil... to act for ourselves... and not to be acted upon... men and women are free according to the flesh, and all things [including problems and crosses] are given them which are expedient... and we are free to choose liberty and eternal life... or captivity and death" (2 Nephi 2:26–27). Our responses to the problems and crosses that accompany mortality become the road maps our journey into immorality and eternal life.

In his book, *Gospel Doctrine*, President Joseph F. Smith wrote, "Our Elder brother... possessed a foreknowledge of all the vicissitudes [i.e. problems and crosses] through which he would have to pass in the mortal tabernacle... IF CHRIST KNEW BEFORE HAND, THEN SO DID WE."[1] We had foreknowledge of the trials and tribulations awaiting us here on earth and we chose to come and suffer them anyway. Why? Because (1) we knew that is how God became God; and (2) we knew that Jehovah, as the implementer of the Father's plan of happiness, would make it possible to repent and overcome the consequences of "blowing it" when we didn't appropriately resolve our problems.

Recall the occasion when Christ encountered the man blind from birth. One well-meaning disciple in an effort to understand the tragic circumstances dealt this unfortunate soul queried, "Who hath sinned—this man or his parents?" reflecting a mortal philosophy of men's notions mingled with scripture, which reasons that since God is good, then the only way to explain pain, misery, and suffering was either the man or his parents had done something evil and the physical affliction is evidence of such behavior. Recall, however, that Jesus taught them the true purpose of this man's condition, namely, "that the powers of God may be manifest" (see John 9:1–3). I have come to the conclusion that in the councils of heaven, Heavenly Father said: "I have an assignment for someone. You will obtain a physical body, but it will have a problem. It will lack the ability to see. It will be blind. You and your parents will have to endure mistreatment, ridicule, ignorance, and neglect from your brothers and sisters who will not remember or understand." I believe that this unattractive assignment was accepted willingly by the man because he was given the assurance that during Christ's mortal ministry, his suffering would be alleviated as a testimony to those who already believed.

One perspective that often gets out of focus is the role of family problems. Consider the following statement by Elder George Q. Cannon, formerly a member of Quorum of the Twelve and the First Presidency,

> I have this belief concerning us that it was arranged before we came here how we should come and through what lineage we should come...I am convinced that it was [foreordained] before I was born that I should come through my parent as I am sure that I stand here.[2]

My understanding of this "foreordination" is that it bestowed as the result of "exceeding great faith" exercised during our premortal life (See Alma 13), including desiring and choosing not to follow after Lucifer, the father of lies who rebelled when the Father said, "I will send the first." The Prophet Joseph Smith also taught that we had some choice as to the time and the family of our mortal sojourn. So, parents and children, we chose each other! Recognition and admission of that fact puts a different perspective on problems and conflicts that arise in family relationships.

Yes, we chose some of our "crosses" to bear. So let's not complain about them since they are tutorials designed specifically to assist us in our quest to become like unto God. If our first thought, prior to expressions of frustrations, anger, or bitterness that bubble to the surface of the natural man and woman, is to remember that most likely we willingly accepted this particular trial in our pre-earth life. Then we can listen for the Spirit's whisper as we ask instead: What's the message for me associated with this problem? What's in this challenge for me? What is the Lord's trying to teach me? How will my response to this problem impact tomorrow, next week, next year, eternity? We had foreknowledge of the trials and tribulations awaiting us on this earth and we chose to come and suffer them anyway. Why? Because (1) we knew that is how God Our Eternal Father became God; and (2) we knew that Jehovah, as the implementer of the plan of had foreknowledge of the trials and tribulations awaiting us on this earth and we chose to come and suffer them anyway.

Reminders That We Are Not Self Sufficient.

Consider the following wisdom penned by Leslie Weatherhead, who reminds us of what our attitude should be when besieged by problems in our daily lives:

> When I am tempted to listen to hot, egotistical voices within my own heart; when it seems that love can never win but always loses; when it seems as though humility is ruthlessly trodden down by those who climb over it on their way to their own selfish ambitions; when it seems as though God cannot possibly triumph; when pity, love, mercy, kindness, and tenderness are weaknesses; when it seems as though greatness is possessed only by those who know how to grab and have the power to snatch at it no matter what the cost to others—yes, when those voices sound in my own heart which say that you must play for your own hand, you must think of number one, you must not let yourself be trodden down—when I am thus tempted, I [remember] the

tinkling of water poured in a basin and see, as in a vision, the Son of God washing the disciples' feet.[3]

Trials and tribulations serve to remind us of our dependency on God, and the need to forget ourselves and focus on serving others so that we might experience the unconditional love of our Elder Brother, Jesus Christ. We recall with sadness the tremendous afflictions endured by Joseph Smith while incarcerated in Liberty Jail. Yet out of that prison-temple emerged three of the most beautiful revelations (Doctrine and Covenants 121, 122, 123) concerning the exercising of priesthood and maintaining personal relationships. While we all rejoice in the triumph of Joseph over those brutal and inhumane conditions, there is another part of the story that has been overlooked, but which contains a significant message for each of us. Sidney Rigdon was released from Liberty Jail approximately two months before the others. He left muttering, "The suffering of Jesus Christ was foolish compared to his."[4] It would not be appropriate for us to render judgment on Sidney Rigdon or any others who complained and murmured from having suffered the atrocities in Missouri. But to assert that Christ's atoning sacrifice, bearing the weight of all the sins of mankind from Adam to the end of the world, and the heart-wrenching pain of our sorrows, grief, and pain was foolishness compared to Rigdon's brief confinement in Liberty Jail smacks of that satanic defiance and arrogance which leads to apostasy. This moment marked a turning point in Sidney's life. After this experience (problem) and his inappropriate response and prideful attitude, he was no longer the distinguished leader he had been in the early years of this dispensation. Soon, Joseph released Elder Rigdon as member of the First Presidency. After the Prophet's death Sidney plotted against the Quorum of the Twelve in an effort to gain control over the Church. In the end, he died a bitter man; one who had lost his faith, his testimony, and perhaps his priesthood blessings.

The Lord has promised us, just as he did Joseph Smith in Doctrine and Covenants 24:8: "Be patient in afflictions [problems] for thou shalt have many; endure them, for I am with thee, even unto the end of thy days." We can also draw strength from Alma's counsel to his son Helaman: "I do know that whosoever shall put their trust in God shall be supported in their trials, and their troubles, and their afflictions" (Alma 36:3). Problems come in many guises; but they serve as celestial memory joggers to remind us of things we previously learned. Humbly seeking the

Lord and his servants allows us be receptive to gentle nudges that foster remembering and understanding of that which we have forgotten.

OPPORTUNITIES—Problems Pull Us Out of Ruts and Cause Us to Think Creatively to Resolve Our Problems.

Too often, we live our lives as though we were on "cruise control" or that a click here and there on a bright little screen will solve our problems. The role of problems is to disrupt our apathy and shake up our comfort zones and raise us to new plateaus of progress. Consider the principle of inertia in physical science. One of its definitions is that an object in motion will tend to stay in motion in the same direction unless acted upon by an external force. Problems are not designed to impede progress, but to re-direct our ruts back to the "straight and narrow path that leads to eternal life" (See 1 Nephi 8:20; 2 Nephi 31:18; 33:9).

President Hugh B. Brown, formerly a counselor to President David O. McKay, once asked the question: "Why was Abraham commanded to offer Isaac to the Lord?" Recall that when Abraham was a young man about the same age as Isaac (twenty-four years old) his father, who had fallen into idolatry in Ur of Chaldees and had become a high priest in the false Babylonian religion, tried to offer up Abraham as a human sacrifice to false Gods. Only through divine intervention was Abraham spared. Thus, Abraham, who abhorred the idolatrous practice of human sacrifice, was now being asked by the Lord to engage in the very act that his idol-worshipping father had unrighteously attempted years earlier. What a test! Here is President Brown's response as to why the test. "Abraham needed to learn something about Abraham."[5] What was that "something"? I believe it was transforming Abraham's desires to align with God, even though he did not understand this particular lesson and its symbolism.

Thinking creatively about our problems and extricating ourselves from the "ruts of stinkin' thinkin'," as a motivational speaker and great friend of mine labeled it, is a fundamental part of being tested as was Abraham. His test was the most difficult things that the Lord could design. Joseph Smith on one occasion said, "That if God could have found a deeper way to test Abraham, he would have used that."[6]

BLESSINGS—Problems Open Doors We Usually Wouldn't Go Through

Among the graduates in the August 1984 commencement exercises at BYU was a thirty-four-year old student from Thailand named Sauan

Sukhan, who received a PhD in sociology. There is nothing extraordinarily startling about that accomplishment except for the personal story of valor, triumph, and courage to open and walk through doors that usually wouldn't have been traversed. Sauan was born in a remote village in Thailand some 350 miles north of Bangkok. To characterize his parents and indeed the entire village, poor is a pathetic understatement. Their home was a shelter constructed of bamboo and grass. At the age of three, Sauan began working full days tending water buffalo and cultivating rice paddies. It is something of a miracle that Sauan survived the myriad of childhood diseases so common to that country. Eight of his fourteen brothers and sister did not. He watched his devout Buddhist parents bury them one by one.

At the village school, there were no textbooks, no library, no paper or pencils; and, of course, there were no such devices as a computer, tablet, or smartphone. Two teachers helped four hundred children practice on slate or dry clay. Only four years of rudimentary education were available in that small village. But Sauan wanted knowledge—as much as he could get. So, from grade 5 through 10, he walked fifteen miles a day to a school in a neighboring village. That was three hours each way in the dry season and considerably longer in the rainy months. His parents spent virtually all of their savings, which you might guess wasn't much for a family whose income was $150 (US) per year, to purchase Sauan a used bicycle so that his daily trek for education might not be so burdensome. They gave him everything they had, and when that was gone they gave him encouragement. But after tenth grade, there was no money for Sauan to go to Bangkok and obtain further education. So, like countless generations of his ancestors, he returned to the water buffalo and rice paddies that would forever mark the boundaries of his very narrow world. But even in the remote corners of rural Thailand, the Spirit of the Lord bears sway. Sauan, with the blessing of his parents, left the village and went to the city, not knowing how long he would be able to stay. And there, in a providential moment, he opened a door, not of an educational institution, but an eternal door where stood two young Americans who had short hair, wore white shirts, and spoke impeccable Thai. The rest is history—sweet history.[7]

I too was nudged in directions I never expected through trials in my life. About six months after my oldest son was born, I lost my job. We moved to Salt Lake City in anticipation of greater prospects for employment. We found a small duplex apartment to which I came home one spring evening commiserating about how tough life was in the constant struggle to provide for a family. While sitting at the dinner table, my wife looked out the window and noticed a neighbor across the alley engaged in repairing the roof of a small detached garage ravaged by the harsh Utah winter storms. The man, about seventy-five years old, was grasping a roll of roofing paper in one arm and just starting to climb a ladder to reach the steeply-sloped roof. Nothing out of the ordinary, except his other arm that he was using to grip the rungs of the ladder was in a cast. Disrupting my soliloquy over the problems facing us, my wife prodded me out the door to offer assistance to this gentleman, who by now I saw was nearing the point of potentially falling and being seriously hurt. I rushed over and grabbed the roll of roofing paper (much to his surprise, since I was a total stranger) and then helped him come back down the ladder to terra firma. At first he was taken aback at my very assertive action, but then realizing his foolish and precarious situation, graciously accepted my assistance.

It turns out that this neighbor was Hamar Reiser, who served for over forty years as President McKay's personal secretary. Because of the loss-of-job problem, a door of unmeasured opportunity opened—spending summer evenings on the Reiser's patio listing to his experiences with a prophet of God. In addition, one Sunday afternoon, the Reisers invited us to come over to meet one of their long-time friends, Sister Wallace Bennett, wife of the late U.S. Senator from Utah. However, her maiden name was Grant. She was the daughter of President Heber J. Grant. More blessings came pouring out from a door of adversity—listening to life events of another prophet, from his daughter. Though we were experiencing a financial trial, we were placed in a position to be spiritually blessed. Reflecting on the problems in our lives, we would all admit that there have been many doors we would not have opened at all unless a loving, all-wise, and perfect Father in Heaven had not placed obstacles in our way, sometime leaving us with the only option of trying a door we didn't want to open.

LESSONS—Each New Challenge Will Educate Our Desires.

When President Russell M. Nelson was a young intern just out of medical school, he had a close friend who interned with him named Don Davis. Don's wife, Netta, had a serious heart condition (a diseased mitral valve damaged in her youth be rheumatic fever). Sadly, as the months went by, Netta's strength ebbed. Her congestive heart failure worsened. Finally, her little body died because of this malfunctioning valve. This was in the days long before the advent of modern surgical techniques that today routinely repair that kind of heart damage. Netta's passing changed Elder Nelson's life. He became determined to not let her suffering be in vain. He joined forces with a small team of researchers at a well-known university in the Eastern USA. Together, they embarked on a project to develop the first artificial heart-lung machine. The intended purpose of this medical device was to allow surgeons to make necessary heart valve repairs while the circulation of the patient's life-sustaining blood would be maintained by the machine they were developing. To make connectors for tubing, Elder Nelson learned glassblowing. He learned how to operate lathes, drill presses, and other equipment required to make the pumps, valves, and cylinders for this delicate medical instrument. He learned about the physiological elements associated with oxygenation of the blood and the necessary conditions for proper blood flow and the rate of oxygen consumption in heart tissue. He learned how to anti-coagulate blood, and then how to reverse the anti-coagulation so that normal clotting would be restored and patients would not bleed to death. He learned the hard way that bacterial contamination could destroy an otherwise successful experiment, which incidentally became the subject of his PhD thesis.

Many years elapsed before President Nelson and his team left the experimental lab and conducted a practical application in an operating room on a real patient. The pioneering road was long and arduous, full of many lessons to be learned. More than eight years went by before their heart-lung machine was successfully used in open-heart surgery. Netta Davis did not die in vain. Her desperate need motivated Elder Nelson as nothing else could. He remembered her on the day that he performed open-heart surgery on President Spencer W. Kimball to save his life. In a very real sense, it was because of Netta's problem that President Nelson was able to save President Kimball. Problems are challenges that teach us. What is still in question is what kind of learners will we be? Elder Neal A. Maxwell put it succinctly:

> In life, the sandpaper of circumstances [problems] often smooths our crustiness and patiently polishes our rough edges. There is nothing pleasant about it, however. And the Lord will go to great lengths in order to teach us a particular lesson and to help us overcome a particular

weakness, especially if there is no other way. In such circumstances, it is quite useless for us mortals to try to do our own sums when it comes to suffering (in the form of problems). We can't make it all add up because we clearly do not have all the numbers. Furthermore, none of us knows much about the algebra of affliction.[8]

Just like trying to explain suffering and pain, attempting to rationalize God's program for educating our desires is an exercise in futility, until He reveals knowledge to us, in His way and time.

EVERYWHERE—No Person or Place Is Excluded from Problems

That this earth, the telestial kingdom, is a garden of problems is clearly understood by all. But perhaps we forget that perspective more than we should. However, we can become better problem-solvers by contemplating the question: "Is there a refuge from the omniscience of problems?" For an answer we turn to the life of Elder John A. Widtsoe, former member of the Quorum of the Twelve, who graduated summa cum laude from Harvard. Elder Widtsoe wrote:

> The temple is a place of revelation—a graduate course in gospel doctrine. And yet he did not divorce that concept from the recognition that the problems you and I have are very practical, very down-to-earth problems. I would rather take my practical problems to the House of the Lord than anywhere else.[9]

In his book, *In A Sunlit Land*, Elder Widtsoe describes a day when, having been frustrated for several months in assimilating a mass of data he had compiled to derive a specific chemical formula, he took his wife to the Logan Temple to forget his failures. While in one of the rooms of that sacred space, there came the very answer he had heretofore failed to discover. Two books on agrarian chemistry grew out of that single insight—a revelation in the temple of God. The temple is not just the union of heaven and earth. It is the key to the mastery of our earth. It is the Lord's graduate course in subduing the earth, i.e., overcoming our problems.

MESSAGES—Problems Warn Us about Potential Disaster—Desire to be Listening

Problems are placed in our way to warn us about more detrimental and serious dangers. Consider the case of Peter on the night he denied any knowledge of the Master, not once but three times in succession. (See

Matthew 26:69–75; Mark 14:66–72; Luke 22:55–62; and John 18:15–18, 25–27). We typically struggle with and are possibly troubled by Peter's lack of commitment to the gospel since he did not rise to the Savior's defense. President Kimball offered an alternative explanation for Peter's behavior. He suggested that that Savior's statement that Peter would deny him three times before the cock crowed was a specific commandment, not a prophecy. Jesus might have been instructing his chief apostle to deny any association with Christ in order to preserve strong leadership for the Church after the Crucifixion and Resurrection. This may not be the correct interpretation, but it is certainly plausible. And though it presented Peter with a faith-testing problem, perhaps a potentially devastating loss to the infant church was averted.[10]

SOLVABLE—No Problem Is Without a Solution

President Harold B. Lee frequently taught that the answers to all our questions, concerns, and problems are contained in the scriptures and writings of modern-day prophets and apostles. Doctrine and Covenants 18:35 says the following, "These words [meaning the scriptures] are not of men… but of me… for it is my voice which speaketh them unto you; for they are given by my Spirit unto to, and by my power you can read them one to another… wherefore you can testify that you have heard my voice and know my words." What better source for finding solutions to our problems?

As a part of my professional career, I was frequently assigned to conduct live continuing education seminars and conferences for CPAs across the USA. On one occasion, I found myself in Louisville, Kentucky (USA). As was frequently the case, there were other speakers at this conference. On this particular day, there was a colleague, who I had heard of but had never met, speaking in the seminar room adjacent to where I was giving my presentation. I took the occasion to introduce myself and expressed a desire to visit and get acquainted during the lunch break. But as circumstances usually happen in these situations, we were both besieged by questions from participants that we were not able to have some private time during lunch. The desired opportunity did not present itself. However, at day's end, we discovered that we both were headed for the airport to fly to the next seminar and found ourselves riding together in the hotel's shuttle bus. We exchanged pleasantries and discussed some matters concerning our CPA profession, which occupied the transit time to the airport. When we arrived at the airport (this was before September 11), we found that both of us had about an hour and a half before our flights departed. We decided to have a real meal instead of "peanut casserole" that would be served on the plane. Steven (my new friend) and I found an empty table toward the back of a restaurant located in the airport concourse, ordered a dinner, and began to chat again.

In response to his question about my family, I told Steve that my oldest son was currently serving a mission for my church in Chile. I had barely shared that information when Steve blurted out, "So you are a Mormon?" I replied that I was. He told me that Michael, his next door neighbor, and fellow professor at Michigan State University was a member of the Church. In fact, Michael's sons and Steve's sons were approximately the same age and had grown up together. Steve then paused. I could tell that something was weighing on him. After what seemed to be a mini eternity, he looked at me with a tear in his eye and a trembling in his voice and asked, "What do Mormons believe about death?" This was certainly an unexpected question especially in light of our having been acquainted for less than half an hour.

Seeing my perplexed look, he explained that Tuesday (today was a Friday) Michael who had taken his sons (as was their fall ritual) deer hunting in Utah in the early fall had fallen asleep at the wheel driving through Nebraska on the way back to Lansing, Michigan (USA) and that Michael's seventeen-year old son had been killed in the accident. Michael was in critical condition in a Nebraska hospital. The funeral for Michael's son was scheduled for the next day—Saturday. Steve looked at me with tears in his eyes and said, "How do I talk to my seventeen-year-old son about death; that his best friend (Michael's son) won't be on the baseball team in the spring; and that they won't graduate together? How do I explain this tragedy to my son?" His despair was overwhelming.

For the next hour, being guided by the Spirit, I told Steve about the plan of happiness—why we are here, where we came from, and what the opportunities are after this mortal experience with all its challenges and problems. As is often the case in these situations, time flew by and we both had to rush to our gates so as not to miss our flights. As we parted, he grabbed my hand, shook it warmly, and thanked me profusely for what I had shared with him. He said that he wished that he had had a tape recorder (before smartphones) available to capture my words so that he could remember what I had explained to him about life and death. I assured him that he would be guided and remember the important ideas that I had taught him which would be most helpful for his son. As he walked away toward his gate, he turned back and reached for my arm to have me face him again. He said something that I will never forget. "Your being here (in Louisville) today was not an accident, was it?" His words sent shivers thru my body. Instantly, the Spirit told me that God had placed me there at that time and place for a reason. I assured him that my being there on that day was not a quirk of fate, nor was it a coincidence. (I don't believe in coincidences, and neither should any member of the Church.) Comforted, he turned and ran to his gate.

This incident, which has been very sacred to me over the years, is even more meaningful in the context of the notion that all problems have a solution. You see, I was scheduled to be in Louisville more than nine months before the accident involving Steve's friend and his son. A loving Father in Heaven knew that Steve would be facing seemingly inexplicable circumstances on that fall day in October and arranged for both of us to be in the same place at the same time so that a solution would be forthcoming for a critical problem in the life of one of His children. A message that this circumstance reinforced is that, there are not such things as "coincidences." When our desires are pure and in line with God's, we will be the tool He uses to help one of His children.

Notes

1. Joseph F. Smith, 8th Edition (Salt Lake City, Deseret Book, 1949), 13.
2. Utah Genealogical and Historical Magazine, Vol. 21, 1930, 24.
3. *Eternal Voices* (New York: Abingdon Press, 1940), 81–82.
4. History of the Church, 3:264.
5. BYU Devotional Address, October 12, 1971.
6. Journal of Discourses 24:264.
7. Adapted from "Education: Unlocking Opportunity," BYU Education Week Address, Barbara Winder, August 16, 1988.
8. *Notwithstanding My Weakness* (Salt Lake City: Bookcraft, Inc. 1986), 67–68.
9. Truman Madsen, *The Highest In Us* (Salt Lake City: Bookcraft, Inc., 1978), 97–98.

10. For President Kimball's full commentary and analysis, see LDS Institute of Religion Manual, The Life and Teachings of Jesus and His Apostles, Appendix D, "Peter, My Brother," 1979, 488–93

CHAPTER 10
Conclusion

If our prayers consist only of words and letters, and do not contain our heart's desires, how can they rise up to God?

—Avodat Halev[1]

Elder Neal A. Maxwell taught, "What we insistently desire, over time, is what we will eventually become and what we will receive in eternity… only by educating and training our desires can they become our allies instead of our enemies!"[2] President Ezra Taft Benson echoed a similar notion, "Daily, constantly, we choose by our desires, our thoughts, our actions, whether we want to be blessed or cursed, happy or miserable."[3] Over the course of our lives, we become more disposed to choose in the direction of past choices. The outcomes of our persistent choices begin to produce the "rewards" of such choices and incline us to choose similarly again. Habits and patterns of behavior are formed and the desires of our hearts become clearer to us. Such clarity may, at times, startle us and give us the necessary impetus to repent or it may simply confirm in us the direction we have chosen to travel. A humorous anecdote involving two men who often spoke of important things drives home the point:

> 1st Man: "Good and evil are like two dogs inside me, vying for dominance, clawing and biting and snarling"
> 2nd Man: "Oh? Which one wins the fight?"
> 1st Man: "The one I feed."

So it is with all of us. Over the course of our lives, we will either nurture those desires that eventually build our eternal character, or not. Elder Neal A. Maxwell counseled,

> Desire denotes a real longing or craving. Hence, righteous desires are much more than passive preferences or fleeting feelings.... there remains an inner zone in which we are sovereign, unless we abdicate. In this zone lies the essence of our individuality and our personal accountability... mostly we become victims of our own wrong desires... like it or not... reality requires that we acknowledge [and accept] responsibility for our desires.[4]

That's a sobering thought. We are continually reminded about accountability for our actions, but it makes perfect sense, in light of the equivalent role of desires and works in the judgment day process, that we are we are also accountable for our desires. And just as our actions are either good or bad, our desires either align with God's or they don't. No grey area! Mormon scholar and author, Kevin Christensen also weighs in on this idea:

> The sacrifice of a broken heart involves putting at risk what we desire. The sacrifice of a contrite spirit involves putting at risk those thoughts we think... these two sacrifices correspond directly to the figures of Fear and Desire which stand as temple guardians in the ancient world. Fear is what we think; Desire is what we want...I once studied over seventy reasons that biblical peoples gave to justify rejection of biblical prophets. Eventually, I realized that they all boiled down to people saying, "It's not what I want (desire)."[5]

A few years ago, I had the privilege of becoming acquainted with the executive director of one of the largest Reform Jewish synagogues in Chicago. At the time, she was in the early stages of also being the caregiver for her husband who had been diagnosed with a debilitating and terminal disease. As I observed the loving kindness she exhibited during the heart-wrenching process of watching a loved one dying a slow death, I was touched by her ability to balance the demands of her career and being a wife. After the funeral was held, I took the opportunity to "sit Shiva," which is the thirty-day period of intensive mourning that Jewish people observe to celebrate the life of loved ones who have died. As you may suspect, there were many who came to express condolences and extend love to her during this difficult time of grief. I noted, however, that she had prepared herself for Shiva. Most people would ask her, "How are you doing?"—a sincere inquiry. Probably, if we were in her shoes, our response would be "I am fine," "I'm okay," or other similar expressions. But to my pleasant surprise and edification, she frequently replied, "*I am doing what matters.*"

May God bless each of us.

To desire to do what matters, because, after all, desires matter!

Notes

1. Avodat Halev, Worship of the Heart: Issac M. Wise Temple, K. K. B'Nai Yeshurun, Cincinnati, Ohio, 2008, 79.
2. Neal A Maxwell, "According to the Desires of [Our] Hearts," *Ensign*, November 1996, 21–22.
3. Ezra Taft Benson, "The Great Commandment—Love the Lord," *Ensign*, May 1988, 6.
4. Neal A Maxwell, "According to the Desires of [Our] Hearts," *Ensign*, November 1996, 21–22.
5. Kevin Christensen, "Hindsight on a Book of Mormon Historical Critique," FARMS Review: Volume 22, Issue 2, 94.

BIBLIOGRAPHY

Anderson, Wilford W. "The Music of the Gospel." *Ensign*, May 2015.

Avodat, Halev. "We Are Becoming." Worship of the Heart. Cincinnati, Ohio: Issac M. Wise Temple, K. K. B'Nai Yeshurun, 2008.

Benson, Ezra T. "Cleansing the Inner Vessel." *Ensign*, May 1986.

_____ "Born of God." *Ensign*, July 1989.

Brown, Hugh B. "This Same Jesus," General Conference, October 12, 1971.

_____. "God Is the Gardener," Commencement Address at BYU May 31, 1968.

Busche, F. Enzio. "Unleashing the Dormant Spirit" Speeches of the Year: 1995–1996: Brigham Young University Press, 1996.

_____, "Truth is the Issue" *Ensign*, November, 1993.

Christensen, Kevin. "Hindsight on a Book of Mormon Historical Critique" FARMS Review Vol. 22 Issue 2, Provo, UT.

Clark, James R. "Messages of the First Presidency of the Church of Jesus Christ of Latter-day Saints, 6 vols." Salt Lake City: Bookcraft, Inc. 1965–75.

Covey, Steve. "The Divine Center" Salt Lake City: Bookcraft, Inc. 1982.

Darwin, Charles. "The Origin of Species."

England, Eugene. "Trouble with Excellence, or How to Value the 'Less Honorable' Gifts" Excellence (Salt Lake City: Deseret Book, 1984).

Farrar, Austin. "Grete Clerk" Light on C. S. Lewis, compiled by Jocelyn Gibb, New York: Harcourt & Brace, 1965.

Ford, Ford Madox. "The Good Soldier" Project Gutenberg EBook, 2013.

Grant, Heber, J. *Juvenile Instructor,* July 1, 1903.

Hales, Robert D. "With All the Feeling of a Tender Parent: A Message of Hope to Families" *Ensign*, May 2004.

_____. "Personal Revelation: The Teachings and Example of the Prophets" *Ensign*, November 2007.

_____ Devotional Address given to the students of BYU on March 15, 1988.

Holland, Jeffrey R. "Miracles of the Restoration" *Ensign*, November, 1994.

_____, "Cast Not Away Your Confidence" Speeches of the Year 1998–1999.

Kimball, Spencer J. "Peter, My Brother," "The Life and Teachings of Jesus and His Apostles" Institute of Religion Manual, 1978, Appendix D.

Lee, Harold B. "Stand Ye in Holy Places" (Salt Lake City, Deseret Book, 1974).

MacDonald, George. "Anthology" New York: MacMillan, 1941.

Madsen, Truman G. "The Highest In Us" (Salt Lake City: Bookcraft, Inc. 1978).

_____. "The Radiant Life" (Salt Lake City: Bookcraft, Inc. 1994).

Maxwell, Neal A. "That Ye May Believe" (Salt Lake City: Bookcraft, Inc., 1992).

_____. "The Education of Our Desires" Address to Students at the LDS Institute of Religion—University of Utah, January 5, 1983.

_____. "For I Will Lead You Along" *Ensign*, May 1988.

_____. Address given at the Annual Banquet of the Foundation for Ancient Research and Mormon Studies (FARMS), September 27, 1991.

_____. "The Disciple-Scholar" Learning in the Light of Faith (Salt Lake City: Bookcraft, Inc. 1995).

_____. "Notwithstanding My Weakness" Salt Lake City: Bookcraft, Inc. 1966.

McGrath, Alister. "Knowing Christ" (New York: Doubleday Galilee, 2002).

_____. "Doubting: Growing through the Uncertainties of Faith" Downers Grove, IL: IVP Books, 2006.

McConkie, Bruce L. "Jesus Christ and Him Crucified" Devotional Speeches of the Year" Provo, UT: Brigham Young University Press, 1976.

Oaks, Dallin H. "Scripture Reading and Revelation" *Ensign*, January, 1995.

Packer, Boyd K. "Teach Ye Diligently" (Salt Lake City: Deseret Book, 1975).

_____. "That All May Be Edified" (Salt Lake City: Bookcraft, Inc. 1982).

Perry, Tom L., "Becoming Self-Reliant." Ensign, November, 1991.

Pratt, Orson. "The Holy Spirit" Orson Pratt: Writings of an Apostle. Salt Lake City: Mormon Heritage Publishers, 1976.

Pearson, Carol Lynn. "The Cast" *The Growing Season*. (Salt Lake City: Bookcraft, Inc. 1976).

Scott, Richard G. "Learning to Recognize Answers to Prayer" *Ensign*, November, 1989.

Smith Jr., Joseph. "Teachings of the Prophet Joseph Smith" Salt Lake City: Desert Book Co.

Smith, Joseph F. *Juvenile Instructor*, 1901.

_____. "Gospel Doctrine—7th Edition" (Salt Lake City: Deseret Book, 1939)

_____."Gospel Doctrine- 8th Edition" (Salt Lake City: Deseret Book, 1949).

Talmage, James E. "Jesus the Christ" (American Fork, Utah: Covenant Communications, Inc. 2006).

Tolkien, J. R. R. "The Lord of the Rings, 3 vol.

Weatherhead, Leslie. "Eternal Voices" (Abingdon Press: New York, 1940).

Widtsoe, John. "Temple Worship" Lecture Given in the Assembly Hall on October 12, 1920.

_____ "The House of the Lord" *Improvement Era*, April, 1936.

Winder, Barbara. BYU Education Week, August 16, 1988.

Young, Brigham. *Deseret News*, September 10, 1859.

_____. "Remarks given April 17, 1853", Journal of Discourses, 26 vols. Liverpool: editor F. D. Richards, 1855.

_____. "Discourse" *Deseret News Weekly*, August 31, 1854.

About the Author

Marlow C. Hunter was born and raised in Wyoming (USA), attended and graduated from Brigham Young University with a BA degree in mathematics, physics, and chemistry, and received a Secondary Education Teaching certificate in 1971. Three years later, he was awarded a Master of Business Administration, majoring in accounting and minoring in economics and finance from the University of North Texas. Seeing employment opportunities available with the large, international public accounting firms, he was hired by Arthur Anderson and completed the requirements to be licensed as a certified public accountant

(CPA). He began his forty-five-year career in Dallas, Texas (USA), where he worked with a variety of companies and organizations to fulfill their financial reporting responsibilities. After five-year stint with Anderson, he joined a colleague to form a CPA firm where he spent the next fifteen years. In 1993, Marlow formed his own CPA firm with offices in Dallas (USA) and Chicago (USA). He has given back to his profession by serving on several volunteer committees, including the Ethics Committee, which oversees CPA's compliance with the Code of Professional Conduct. His training in education became another way by which he serves the CPA community. In 1988, continuing professional education (CPE) became mandatory for CPAs in the USA. Over the last thirty years, Marlow has designed, developed, and written dozens of CPE seminars, as well as given hundreds of educational presentations, both in live and webcast formats, to thousands of CPAs.

Even more significant than his forty-year commitment to his profession is his dedication and devotion to The Church of Jesus Christ of Latter-day Saints. He has served as a counselor to three bishops, as a bishop, high councilor, temple ordinance worker, and as a part-time institute instructor. For the last twelve years, Marlow has been teaching a stake-wide Adult Gospel Education class.

Marlow lives in Chicago (USA). He and his wife have six children and eighteen grandchildren.